MW01178313

BELGRADE

Complete guide for getting by in Belgrade

Prospekt der Stadt Belgrad in Servien.

First Edition, August 2006

Nemanja Tasić, Slobodan Đuričić

How to Conquer Belgrade

First Edition, September 2006

"But you arise, beneath the shining star of dawn,
With Avala's blue distant mountain far below.
You glitter, when the stars have faded with the morn,
Then, sun-like, melt the ice of tears and last year's snow.
In you there is no empty vanity or death.
You glisten like an unearthed sword from bygone years.
In you is all revived, set dancing, given breath,
Renewed, refreshed, like bright day and like children's tears.
And when my voice, and eyes, and breath are stilled at last,
About me you will fold your arms and hold me fast."

Miloš Crnjanski "Lament over Belgrade"
(extract, © Miloš Crnjanski Foundation)

The publisher does not bear any responsibilities for the changes in addresses,
telephone numbers, prices or any other
data, that took place after the publication
of this guide. The publisher does not bear
responsibilities for any consequences
arising from the use of this guide. All rec-
ommendations were made on the basis of
personal experience and pleasure. No one
mentioned in this guide paid to be adver-
tised. Commercial advertisements are only put on the enclosed map of Belgrade.
No one deliberatly posed for a photo-
graph. They were not retouched, apart
from the correction of contrast and composition.

If you have any suggestions or comments
or you need help (free of charge) or advice on planning a trip to Belgrade, contact us on the e-mail address:
belgrade.guide@gmail.com

The guide can be ordered over the Internet presentation www.beligrad.com

Editor: Slobodan Đuričić

Text: Nemanja Tasić

Photographs: Jelena Tasić
(apart form those marked with an asterisk -
received from the establishments mentioned)

Design and preparation for print:
Viktor Perolo, Tanja Bačikin

Sketches: Momo Kapor

Translation into English: Jovana Popović

Translation into Spanish:
Marija Milićević, Jelena Knežević

Translation into German:
Jovana Trifunović

Translation into French: Jelena Miljković

Translation into Slovenian: Bojana Balon

Translation into Italian:
Aleksandra De Lorenzis

Resources:
"Beograd ispod Beograda",
Zoran Lj. Nikolić & Dr Vidoje D. Golubović,
Službeni list SCG, 2004
"Muzej grada Beograda", grupa autora,
Muzej grada Beograda, 2003
www.serbia-tourism.org
www.biojednomjedanbeograd.com

Acknowledgements:
Momo Kapor
Bratislav Petković
Museum of Yugoslav Film Archives
Serbian Railways

Print: GRAFOLIK Belgrade

Number of copies: 4000

ISBN 86-83253-02-3

CONTENTS

CONTENTS

Food and Drink **60**

Night-life **78**

Useful Information **106**

Two Days in Belgrade **140**

Belgrade Women **92**

Traffic **96**

СТАСИЄВИЋЬ СВОМЬ ОТЕЧЕСТВУ.

Position and climate

Belgrade

Belgrade is located in the place where the strong Danube kisses the wild Sava, on the border between the east and the west, where beutiful girls with misterious eyes are born. It is one of the oldest cities in Europe. Because of its position on the intersection of roads, on the place where civilisations clashed, it was completely demolished 40 times, like no other capital. The name of Belgrade means "White City". It was also called "the mount for thinking", "the house of wars" and "sin city". Le Corbusier said that it was the ugliest city on the most beautiful spot. Besides Constantinople, Belgrade is the only city dedicated to the Most Holy Virgin.

You can find out more about the origin and history of Belgrade on page 33

You can find out more about the origin and history of Belgrade on page 33

Position

Belgrade is the capital of Serbia and has about 2 million inhabitants. It is situated in south-eastern Europe, on the Balkan penninsula, at the crossroads of routes that connect Western and Central Europe with the Aegean and Black Sea, Turkey and the Near East. Its coordinates are: 44°49'14" North geographic latitude and 20°27'44" East geographic longitude, 116m above sea-level (city centre, middle of Knez Mihailova Street). Time zone is Central European - CET (GMT+1 hour).

The summer daylight saving time is from the end of March to the end of October (GMT+2 hours).

Official language is Serbian, Cyrillic script, although Latin script is equally used. Political system is a

parlamentary democracy. Main religion is Christian - Orthodox. Serbian Orthodox Church has been autocephalous since 1219.

It blows most frequently in autumn and winter, in intervals from one to seven days. Whatever you put on in those days, when Košava is blowing, it will not save you from the cold. The rescue is most often sought in bars.

Climate

Climate is mildly continental. Summers are very hot (temperature reaches 38°C), and winters are cold (to -10°C). The snow blanket averages 30-45 days, and its average thickness is 14-25cm. Spring is short and changeable, and autumn with longer sunny and warm periods. Rain is the heaviest in May and June, and the lightest in February. One-day rainfalls are the most common. Bad weather comes from the west and south-east wind "Košava", brings fine and dry weather.

How to get to Belgrade

By plane

"Nikola Tesla" Airport is situated 18km west of the city centre, near the place called Surčin. National airline is JAT Airways and it is one of the safest airlines in the world. Stewardesses are a bit older than average in the world but, on the other hand, more experienced. Direct flights to European cities: Amsterdam, Athens, Basel, Berlin, Brussels, Copenhagen, Düsseldorf, Frankfurt, Göteborg, London, Ljubljana, Milan, Munich, Moscow, Paris, Prague, Rome, Sarajevo, Skopje, Stockholm, Stuttgart, Tirana, Vienna, Zurich. Belgrade is linked with the whole world through the connected flights of foreign airlines.

Transport from the airport to the city:

1. JAT AIRWAYS BUS

Bus route: Airport - New Belgrade (Fontana) - Central railway station - Slavija square. Fare: 160 dinars*.

The buses go in both directions, once before and once after every flight. Departures from Slavija terminal 5am-9pm. Departures of the bus from the "Nikola Tesla" Airport: 7am-10pm. The journey takes 30 minutes.

> *At the time the guide was witten 1 euro was worth 87 dinars.

➔ More information on money exchange on page 110.

2. BUS GSP

(public city transport)

Bus 72. Bus ticket can be bought in the bus itself and costs 60 dinars. The bus goes to the city centre (Zeleni venac).

➔ More information on city transport on page 104.

3. TAXI

Avoid the taxi drivers who stand outside the very terminal and solicit passengers, since they will try to charge you much more by driving without turning on the meter. It is best to ring the taxi by phone (or ask someone to do that for you) and your vehicle will arrive in 10-15 minutes. It takes 20 minutes to the centre and the fare is not over 10 euros. The number of passengers and luggage do not influence the fare. Taxi firms we recommend are:

Lux taxi - Tel: (+38111) 3033-123, (+38165) 3033-123 and (+381) 3033 for the ring by SMS*

Beotaxi - Tel: (+38111) 970 and (+381) 9700 for the ring by SMS*

NBA taxi - Tel: (+38111) 3185-777

> *You ring a taxi by SMS by typing the following text: **Medjunarodni dolasci aerodrom** (International arrivals Airport) and send it to the desired number. You will receive an answer: **vozilo XXX za X minuta** (vehicle XXX in X minutes). Go outside and wait for your taxi.

➔ More information on taxi transport on page 98.
➔ More information on making phone calls on page 111.

4. RENT-A-CAR

Offices at the airport:

AVIS-AUTOTEHNA
Tel: (+38111) 2286-133;
info@autotehna.com;

www.avis.co.yu

Budget - Tel: (+38111) 2286-361; www.budget.co.yu

Hertz - Tel: (+38111) 2286-017; reservation@hertz.co.yu; www.hertz.co.yu

Primero - Tel: (+38111) 2286-362; 063-474-121 (0-24h); www.primero.co.yu

Škoda-Kole - Tel: (+38111) 2286-360; www.skoda-kole.co.yu

YU Tim - Tel: (+38111) 2286-161; www.yutim.co.yu

5. LIMO SERVICE

Elite Limo: the longest limousine in Europe (Cadillac Mirage 130 - 11m), 100 EUR/hour*; Tel: (+38163) 595-952, (+38121) 458-838; e-mail: office@limo.co.yu

Limo service: 30-70 EUR/hour* (Cadillac, Linkoln);

Tel: (+38163) 1235-555; e-mail: mobilsis@drenik.net

Limo City Line: 10 EUR* (Peugeot 607, 807, BMW 5); Tel/Fax: (+38111) 3011-242, (+38163) 253-315; e-mail: office@limoservice.co.yu

---

The prices shown are for the transport from the airport to the city.

Useful telephone numbers and addresses:

➜ *More information on making phone calls on page 111.*

"Nikola Tesla" Airport - Tel: 2094-444, 2094-000

Lost luggage - Tel: 2676-374 (JAT Airways), 2286-411 (other airlines)

Reception of VIP passengers Tel: 2097-026; Fax: 2286-440 www.airport-belgrade.co.yu

JAT info telephone: 3112-123; www.jat.com

JAT offices:

Bulevar Kralja Aleksandra 17, Tel: 3232-372, 3231-042

Kralja Milana 18, Tel: 2643-997, 2686-964

"Slavija" Hotel, Svetog Save 1-9, Tel: 450-584, 450-562

Bulevar umetnosti 16 (Novi Beograd), Tel: 2139-088

"Nikola Tesla" Airport, departures counter, Tel: 2097-348, 2097-462

JAT Cargo (freight transport) - Tel: 2010-130, 2010-240

Offices of foreign airlines:

AEROFLOT (Russia), Knez Mihailova 30/III, Tel: 3286-071, 2097-244 (Airport); www.aeroflot.ru

AEROSVIT (Ukraine), Nikole Spasića 10, Tel: 3283-430; www.aerosvit.com

AIR FRANCE (France), Knez Mihailova 30/II, Tel: 2638-222, 2286-481 (Airport); www.airfrance.com

ALITALIA (Italy), Terazije 43/I, Tel: 3245-000, 2286-244 (Airport); www.alitalia.com

AUSTRIAN AIRLINES (Austria), Terazije 3/III, Tel: 3248-077, 2286-142 (Airport); www.austrianairlines.co.yu

BRITISH AIRWAYS (G. Britain), Knez Mihailova 30/IV, Tel: 3281-303, 2286-026 (Airport); ww.britishairways.com

CZECH AIRLINES (Czech Republic), Kralja Milana 6/I, Tel: 3614-590, www.czechairlines.com

EMIRATES (U.A.E.), Knez Mihailova 6/VI, Tel: 624-435, www.emirates.com

LUFTHANSA (Germany), Terazije 3/VII, Tel: 3034-944, 2286-142 (Airport); www.lufthansa .co.yu

MALEV (Hungary), Knez Mihailova 30/II, Tel: 2626-377; www.malev.hu

OLYMPIC AIRLINES (Greece), Vase Čarapića (Vasina) 14/I, Tel: 3036-850, 2286-274 (Airport); www.olympicairlines.com

SWISS (Switzerland), Terazije 3/III, Tel: 3030-140, 2286-142 (Airport); www.swiss.com

TUNISAIR (Tunis), Skadarska 19, Tel: 3233-174; www.tunisair.com

Aviotaxi – airplane renting:

JAT Aviotaksi, Vršac; Tel: (+38113) 830-185, (+38163) 248-847; 24h

AVIOGAMA, Veljka Dugoševića 41; Tel: (+38111) 772-130, 771-319

PRINCE AIR, Francuska 35; Tel: (+38111) 3032-303, Fax: 3032-305; www.princeaviation.com

SHUTTLE AIR, "Nikola Tesla" Airport; Tel: (+38111) 3191-771

Low cost airlines:

GERMANWINGS (Bonn-Belgrade) Monday, Wednesday, Saturday www.germanwings.com

Distance of Belgrade from some European cities:

Amsterdam	1760 km
Athens	1090 km
Vienna	621 km
Berlin	1489 km
Brussels	1702 km
Budapest	383 km
Istanbul	928 km
Copenhagen	2018 km
London	2073 km
Ljubljana	528 km
Munich	1020 km
Moscow	2211 km
Oslo	2577 km
Prague	901 km
Roma	1280 km
Stockholm	2622 km

Locations of important sights in the city are marked by tourist signposts in English. Other signposts are in Serbian but in Latin script.

By car

Belgrade is situated on the inter-section of European roads E-70 and E-75. It is an ideal spot for one- or two-day stopover when you are travelling to Greece or Turkey. However, some have stopped for one day and stayed much longer... Foreign drivers in Serbia and Montenegro need inter-national driving licence, vehicle li-cence and insurance policy. You cannot miss the entrance to Belgrade since the motorway runs through the very city (a bypass is still under construction).

Insurance

Valid insurance policies are those from the "Vehicle Insurance Convention" signatory countries. Citizens of other countries have to buy the insurance policy on enter-ing Serbia and Montenegro. The policy is not charged by customs but by the Automobile Association (*Auto-moto savez*).

Traffic accidents

In case of a traffic accident Traffic police should be called (Tel: 92) and they will make a record of the traffic accident. For the vehicles with foreign plates it is necessary to get a confirmation of vehicle damage from the police, which should be shown at the border on leaving Serbia and Montenegro.

"Help-information" Service (Tel: 987, 00-24h) of Automobile Associ-ation of Serbia and Montenegro is available for giving tourist assistance and hauling damaged vehicles.

International tourist-information centre, Tel: 9800 (00-24h) - infor-mation in foreign languages also. www.amsj.co.yu

Road-toll

For passenger vehicles with for-eign plates road-toll is paid on the following sections of the mo-torway through Serbia:

Subotica - Novi Sad: 430 dinars*
Novi Sad - Beograd: 430 dinars
Šid - Beograd: 520 dinars
Beograd - Niš: 1130 dinars
Niš - Leskovac: 260 dinars

> *At the time the guide was witten
> 1 euro was worth 87 dinars.

Fuel

On the main roads and in larger towns some petrol stations work non-stop.

The price of fuel is not over 1 eu-ro a litre. Types of fuel:
- 95-98 octane (super)
- unleaded 95 octane (bmb or be-zolovni)
- 86 octane (premium)
- diesel D2 and EURO diesel (dizel)
- liquid petroleum gas (on lar-ger petrol stations)

Petrol stations which are open 24 hours a day are marked on our map of Belgrade.

Traffic regulations

Speed limit in the residential areas is 60 km/h, if it is not regulated differently by a traffic sign.

On the roads outside towns speed limits are: 120 km/h on the motorway, 100 km/h on main roads, 80 km/h on other roads. Police checks speeding on several places along the main roads.

A child under 12 and an intoxicated person must not sit in the front seat of a passenger vehicle. Allowed quantity of alcohol in the blood of a driver is 0.05%. The use of belts is obligatory for the driver and a passenger sitting on the seat next to the driver. Drivers and passengers on motorbikes are obliged to wear protective helmets while driving (in towns also). It is obligatory to turn on the lights on the motorbikes while driving during the day and the night.

Camping is permitted only at campsites. Vehicles with foreign plates need to have a proper label of the country they are registered in. Police does not treat the foreign citizens differently. If the offence you commit is minor and you have a penitent expression on your face you will get away with a warning, otherwise, you will pay a fine. Do not try to bribe the policemen since that is against the law and you can complicate your vacation.

Detailed information on driving a car in Belgrade on page 99.

Distance of Belgrade from the main border crossings:

MAĐARSKA - Horgoš: 203 km

MAĐARSKA - Kelebija: 190 km

RUMUNIJA - Vatin: 100 km

BUGARSKA - Gradina: 335 km

MAKEDONIJA - Preševo: 391 km

R. SRPSKA - Badovinci: 118 km

HRVATSKA - Batrovci: 113 km

By train

In the past, in the times of Orient Express, travelling by train was the most beautiful way to get to Belgrade. Today the situation is a bit different since train is the slowest means of transport in Serbia. Tracks have not yet been modernised in order to be able to support high-speed trains. Train departures are mainly on time, while the arriving trains can be late. The building of the Central railway station was built in 1884 and is near to the city centre.

From the station to the other parts of the city you can go by taxi (the

same rules apply as to the airport – it is best to call a taxi by phone and not to accept the offers of unlicensed taxi drivers to give you a ride for the fare fixed in advance), or by trams of the public city transport. A ticket is bought on the news-stand (it costs 27 dinars*) or in the vehicle itself from the driver for 40 dinars. Trams 7 and 9 go towards New Belgrade (the stop is on the other side of the street opposite the Railway station), or towards Bulevar Kralja Aleksandra (7) and Vo-ždovac (9) across Slavija square and Saint Sava's Temple (the stop is on the traffic island closer to the Central railway station).

If you are in the mood for a 300m walk up-hill, along Balkanska Street

you can get to the very centre of the city, to Terazije.

> *At the time the guide was witten 1 euro was worth 87 dinars.

→ *More information on getting a taxi on page 98.*
→ *More information on city transport on page 104.*

Useful telephone numbers and addresses:

Serbia Rail, Nemanjina 6;
Tel: 3616-722, Fax: 3616-802;
www.yurail.co.yu

Central railway station – information,
Tel: 2645-822, 2641-488 (00-24h)

Car on train and couchette,
Tel: 3235-400

Train ticket vendors:

KSR, M. Milovanovića 5; Tel: 2643-388

PUTNIK, Dragoslava Jovanovića 1;
Tel: 3231-905

PUTNIK, Terazije 27; Tel: 3230-282

PUTNIK KMG, Karađorđeva 83;
Tel: 3614-787

WASSTELS, Savski trg 2;
Tel: 2658-868

REKREATURS, Dragoslava Jovano-vića 3; Tel: 3230-535

PUTNIK, Zemun, Glavna 24;
Tel: 2614-516

→ *More information on making phone calls on page 111.*

Fares in international traffic:

INTER RAIL

(a type of pass that enables travelling on the whole railway network of 29 European countries and Morocco, as well as on the lines of the shipping agency AND/HLM). Rail fares (EUR):

type of PASS	valid	to the age of 26	adults	children aged 4-12
one zone	16 DAYS	136, 50	200, 20	100, 10
two zones	22 DAYS	192, 50	277, 20	138, 60
global	1 MONTH	269, 50	382, 20	191, 10

WIEN SPECIAL

Return-ticket Belgrade - Vienna:
II class - 61 euro,
I class - 101 euro.

By coach

Belgrade coach station is situated right next to the Central railway station, near the city centre. Arrival terminals are separated from the very station and situated across the street, in the park. Belgrade is connected by regular lines (during summer additional ones also) with all major cities in Serbia and Montenegro. Possibilities for getting from the station to other parts of the city are the same as from the Railway station (see previous section).

Information and reservations:

Local lines -
Tel: 2636-299 (5:30-22h)

International lines - BAS turist,
Tel: 2658-759 (7-20h)

Ticket vending 00-24h;
www.bas.co.yu

We recommend the busses of "Lasta" Traffic Company, member of EUROLINES system:

International traffic -
Tel: 2653-053, 2627-146
www.eurolines.co.yu

→ More information on making phone calls on page 111.

DOBRO DOŠLI ~ WELCOME
WILLKOMMEN ~ BIENVENUE

Some of the international coach lines:

Amsterdam, Florence, Malmö, Stuttgart, Athens, Frankfurt, Milan, Verona, Basel, Göteborg, Munich, Zagreb, Vienna, Graz, Montpellier, Geneva, Berlin, Hamburg, Paris, Bratislava, Innsbruck, Prague, Brussels, Istanbul, Salzburg, Budapest, Copenhagen, Sofia, Zurich, Lyon, Thessalonica, Dortmund, Ljubljana, Stockholm.

By ship

Belgrade was built on the banks of two international rivers – the Danube and the Sava. Down the Danube and the channel Rhine-Main-Danube you can even get to Belgrade by ship from the North or Black sea. 588km of international waterway on the Danube run through Serbia. Internal border crossings are in Apatin, Novi Sad and Belgrade. There are no regular passenger lines in Serbia and for that reason you can reach Belgrade only by foreign tourist ships that cruise down the Danube or by your own yacht.

Although many Belgraders spend all their free time on water (on boats and rafts), nautical infrastructure is not developed enough. It will be difficult to find an available berth, and it will be impossible to find electrical and water supply, showers, fuel, service and shops in one place. Forget about buying a map of the Danube or a pilot book.

River policemen are kind but not very fluent in foreign languages. Most of these shortcomings will be compensated by the hospitality of Belgraders who will help you get by, buy supplies, find out the weather forecast and a mechanic if you need one.

> *Places for tying up boats are marked on our map of Belgrade.*

Useful telephone numbers and addresses:

Harbour Master's Office of Belgrade Quay: on the Sava below Kalemegdan, near Brankov Bridge, Tel: (+38111) 2625-977

Yugoslav River Shipping: Kneza Miloša 82, Tel: (+38111) 3617-040; www.jrb.co.yu

Belgrade Port (cargo traffic): Francuska 81
Tel: (+38111) 2751-255;
www.port-bgd.co.yu

Tourist transport by boats (sightseeing or hiring for business meetings, parties, etc.):

Tourist Organisation of Belgrade, www.tob.co.yu

"Putnik" Travel Agency, www.putnik.com

➔ *More information on making phone calls on page 111.*

Visas and Customs Regulations

For the citizens of the following countries visa is not necessary for a stay up to 90 days: Andorra, Argentina, Australia, Belgium, Belarus, Bolivia, Bosnia and Herzegovina, Bulgaria, Czech Republic, Chile, Denmark, Estonia, Finland, France, Greece, Holland, Croatia, Ireland, Island, Italy, Israel, Japan, Canada, Cyprus, Costa Rica, Cuba, Lithuania, Lichtenstein, Latvia, Luxemburg, Hungary, Macedonia, Malta, Monaco, Germany, Norway, New Zealand, Poland, Portugal, Republic of Korea, Romania, USA, San Marino, the Seychelles, Singapore, Slovakia, Slovenia, Spain, Switzerland, Sweden, Tunisia, Vatican, Great Britain.

For the citizens of countries which are not on this list: visas cannot be obtained on the border but should be obtained in the Consulate of Serbia before the journey.

Foreign nationals have to register themselves within 12 hours upon arrival, in the nearest police station in the municipality they are staying in. This will be carried out by the hotel you are staying in or by the friends you are staying with. If you come alone and rent a flat, be sure to register yourself, since the fine for unregistered stay is extremely high.

Credit cards and cash (foreign currency, dinars and Traveller's Cheques) worth up to 2000 EUR can be brought in or out of the country by foreign and native nationals and do not have to be declared. Larger amounts (if you do not intend to spend them in Belgrade) have to be declared at the customs on entering the country. A customs officer will issue a receipt which enables you to freely take out your money when leaving the country. Otherwise, amount larger than 2000 EUR will be temporarily taken when leaving the country and appropriate proceedings will be started (a hassle you want to avoid). It is not allowed to bring more than 120,000 dinars (CSD) into the country without a bank receipt of purchase.

Foreign nationals who have an account with one of the banks in Belgrade are free to take out their money with the receipt of money retrieval. Securities that were obtained accor-ding to the regulations can freely be taken out of the country.

Bans and restrictions

Physical persons cannot import and

sued on the approval of the republic Institute for Cultural Heritage Conservation.

Hunting weapons and ammunition (in a certain amount) can be temporarily brought into Serbia when a person is going into an organized hunt (organised by the Hunting Association or other authorised organisations). Hunters-tourists can take the hunted game and game trophies out of the country only if a certificate was issued (for game), i.e. a trophy certificate (for trophies).

The obligations of foreign nationals who plan a longer stay in Serbia, as

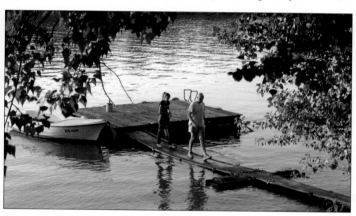

export merchandised goods, weapons and ammunition. Gold in crude or processed shape must not be taken out of the country. When importing animals it is necessary to submit a health-check certificate (done in the country the person is coming from) and to acquire, on the border, a certificate of a carried out veterinary-sanitary control.

Items of artistic or cultural value can be exported – taken out of the country only with the permission of the Ministry for economic relations with foreign countries, which is is-

well as the list of necessary documents, can be found on the Internet site of the Ministry of foreign affairs www.mfa.gov.yu

Detailed information on customs regulations can be found on the Internet site www.fcs.yu
For registration, extension of the stay or solving problems, such as the loss of passport, contact the Head office of Belgrade police - Foreign Nationals ' Department: Bulevar Despota Stefana 107, Tel: 3292-622.

➜ *More information on making phone calls on page 111.*

Accommodation

Accommodation

Hotels that we recommend in this guide offer excellent accommodation and service according to their category. There are many smaller hotels in middle category and with affordable night's accommodation in the city centre. However, in view of some shortcomings (necessary renovation), they are not mentioned here.

Regarding its size and developed congress tourism Belgrade has less luxury hotels than it is necessary and that is why it is best to book your accommodation in advance. The safest way to book

backpackers and the others who find this type of accommodation suitable can use student and school residences listed in our guide (during school holidays, mainly in summer).

accommodation is by phone or fax because in some hotels they do not check their e-mail for some days.

Belgrade got its first real hostels only recently. Apart from them,

List of recommended hotels:
(In alphabetical order)

ALEKSANDAR PALAS *****

City centre, very close to Knez Mihailova Street and Kalemegdan. Luxury little hotel. "Kraljevina" Restaurant with traditional cuisine and café-bar "¿Que Pasa?" with pleasant atmosphere and South American cuisine are inside the hotel complex.

Kralja Petra 13-15; Tel: 3305-300, Fax: 3305-334; e-mail: aleksandar@legis.co.yu; www.aleksandarpalas.com

Rates: App no. 1-8 260 EUR, daily 120 EUR, weekend 220 EUR; App no. 9 (duplex) 360 EUR, daily: 120 EUR, weekend 320 EUR. Tax: included in the price. Breakfast: American breakfast, included in the price. Transfer to airport included in the price.

Cards: Diners Club, Visa, Master Card

Facilities: restaurant, café, café-bar club, exchange office, summer garden, fitness centre, view, lift, wake-up service, room service, available notebook, video conference possibility, massage 24 hours a day, solarium.

Rooms: air-conditioning, satellite TV, Internet access, DVD, radio, mini bar, safe box.

BELGRADE INTER-CONTINENTAL *****

Large, luxury hotel, situated in New Belgrade inside the "Sava" Congress centre complex. Near the motorway (15 minutes from the airport), Belgrade arena and rafts on the Sava-Danube confluence, 5 minutes by car from the city centre.

Vladimira Popovića 10; Tel: 2204-204, Fax: 3111-330; e-mail: ihcbegha@eunet.yu; www.ichbg.com

Rates: 1/1 175 EUR, 1/2 185 EUR, App 290-390-800 Tax: not included in the price (100 dinars/day*). Breakfast: Buffet, included in the price.

Cards: Diners Club, Visa, Master Card, Traveller's Cheques.

Facilities: 2 restaurants, piano bar, pastry shop, night club, car park, garage (paid separately), conference rooms (20-750 seats), business centre, gift shop, exchange office, fitness centre, swimming pool, tennis courts, lift, room service, wake-up service, non-smokers' rooms, Internet access. Rooms: air-conditioning, satellite TV, mini bar, hair-dryer.

BEST WESTERN Hotel M ****

It is situated in a peaceful district, near the motorway and football stadiums of "Red Star" and "Partizan", 15 minutes by car from the city centre. It is famous for good service which attracts a large number of regular customers.

Bulevar Oslobođenja 56a; Tel: 3090-401, Fax: 3090-403; e-mail: office@hotel-m.com; www.hotel-m.com

Rates: 1/1 57 EUR, 1/2 114 EUR, App 185 EUR. Tax: included in the price. Breakfast: buffet, included in the price.

Cards: Diners Club, Visa, Master Card

Facilities: restaurant, bar, car park (paid separately), exchange office, conference rooms (up to 250 seats), business centre, room service, non-smokers' rooms, most rooms look onto the woods. Rooms: air-conditioning, satellite TV, Internet, mini bar, hair-dryer.

BEST WESTERN Hotel ŠUMADIJA ****

On Banovo brdo, 8km from the city centre. Near Ada Ciganlija and Košutnjak. Excellent service, recently renovated to suit business customers.

Šumadijski trg 8 (near Ada Ciganlija on Banovo brdo, 5km from the city centre); Tel: 3054-100, Fax: 3554-368; e-mail: office@hotelsumadija.com; www.hotelsumadija.com

Rates: 1/1 75-99 EUR, 1/2 85-109 EUR, App 125-159 EUR. Taxses: not included in the price. (100 dinars/day). Breakfast: buffet, included in the price.

Cards: Diners Club, Visa, Master Card, DinaCard.

Facilities: café-bar, restaurant, restaurant-garden with 100 seats, business centre, conference rooms. Rooms: air-conditioning, satellite TV, radio, Internet, mini bar, safe box, hair-dryer.

HYATT REGENCY *****

Second largest luxury hotel in Belgrade, situated between the "Sava" Congress centre and the "Ušće" business centre. The most expensive hotel, monotonous food (except in "Focaccia" Restaurant).

Milentija Popovića 5; Tel: 3011-182, Fax: 3112-234; e-mail: belgrade.regency@hyattintl.com; www.regency.belgrade.hyatt.com

Rates: 1/1 295 EUR, 1/2 315 EUR, App 305-400. Tax: not included in the price (100 dinars/day). Breakfast: buffet, not included in the price (20 EUR).

Cards: Diners Club, Visa, American Express, Master Card

Facilities: restaurants, café, tea house, car park (paid separately), night club, fitness centre with swimming pool, conference rooms, business centre, lift, wake-up service, non-smokers' rooms, room service. Rooms: air-conditioning, TV and mini bar.

LE PETIT PIAF ***

Small hotel with home atmosphere in the heart of the bohemian quarter Skadarlija. French restaurant inside the hotel.

Skadarska 34; Tel: 3035-252, Fax: 3035-353; e-mail: office@petitpiaf.com; www.petitpiaf.com

Rates: 1/1 151 EUR, 1/2 181 EUR, App 184-220 EUR. Tax: included in the price. Insurance: not included in the price (100 dinars/day). Breakfast: à la carte, included in the price.

Cards: Visa, Master Card, Maestro.

Facilities: bar, restaurant, terrace, summer garden. Rooms: air-conditioning, cable TV, Internet access, safe box, direct phone line.

MAJESTIC ****

The very centre of the city, café zone on Obilićev venac. Small and agreeable hotel with traditionally good and discreet service, opened in 1937.

Obilićev venac 28; Tel: 3285-777, Fax: 3284-995; e-mail: majestic@eunet.yu; www.majestic.co.yu

Rates: 1/1 65 EUR, 1/2 75-100 EUR, App 120-150 EUR. Tax: included in the price. Breakfast: English, included in the price.

Cards: Diners Club, Visa, Master Card, EuroCard.

Facilities: restaurant, café, summer terrace, garage (paid separately), conference rooms (up to 50 seats each), wake-up service, room service, lift, non-smokers' rooms. Rooms: air-conditioning, TV, mini bar, Internet access.

MOSKVA ****

Elegant hotel on Terazije (the very centre of the city), built in 1907.

The building is under the protection of the state. Rooms are furnished with authentic period furniture and rich collection of paintings. It is unique for having 40 duplexes. The only hotel outside Russia bearing this name.

Balkanska 1; Tel: 2686-255, Fax: 2688-389; e-mail: hotelmoskva@absolutok.net; www.hotelmoskva.co.yu

Rates: 1/1 55 EUR, 1/2 92-102 EUR, App 220-250 EUR. Tax: included in the price. Breakfast: English, included in the price.

Cards: Diners Club, Visa, Master Card, DinaCard.

Facilities: restaurant, bar, breakfast room, banquet hall (up to 50 seats), café on the terrace, pastry shop, Internet access, exchange office, hairdresser's, beauty parlour, room service, wake-up service. Rooms: mini bar and TV, air-conditioning, hair-dryer.

PALACE ****

The hotel with the traditionally good service and regular customers, opened in 1923. Situated in a quiet side street in the city centre, a couple of minutes walk from Knez Mihailova Street and Kalemegdan. Beautiful view over the city from the national restaurant on the last floor. The hotel is the integral part of catering school.

Topličin venac 23; Tel: 2185-585, Fax: 184-458; e-mail: office@palacehotel.co.yu

Rates: 1/1 60 EUR, 1/2 80 EUR, App 100 EUR. Tax: included in the price. Breakfast: buffet, included in the price.

Cards: Diners Club, Visa, Master Card, Maestro.

Facilities: 2 restaurants, bar, conference halls with 150, 50 and 30 seats, garage (paid separately), exchange office, lift, room service, wake-up service, Internet access, hairdresser's. Rooms: satellite TV, mini bar, hair-dryer.

PRESIDENT ★★★★

This small, luxury hotel is situated 12km from the city centre, in the sports centre Kovilovo (the best shooting ranges in Europe). Isolated from the noise of the city, the complex spreads over 26ha of parks and grasslands, surrounded by 100ha of woods (ideal for birdwatching). The complex comprises six shooting galleries, a shop selling sports and hunting equipment, school of shooting, boxes for dogs.

Zrenjaninski put 170; Tel: 2075-200, Fax: 2075-260; e-mail: office@bgsck.org.yu; www.president-belgrade.com

Rates: 1/1 85 EUR, 1/2 90 EUR. Tax: included in the price. Breakfast: buffet.

Cards: Diners Club, Visa, Master Card, Maestro.

Facilities: restaurant, snack-bar, outdoor swimming pool, sports grounds, sauna, fitness centre, conference room, business centre, room service. Rooms: air-conditioning, TV, Internet, safe box, mini bar.

ROYAL ★★★

City centre, close to Kalemegdan and Knez Mihailova Street. Small hotel, modest service, the oldest on the list of the recommended ones (opened in 1886), famous for the cheap restaurant open 24 hours a day.

Kralja Petra 56; Tel: 2626-426, Fax: 2634-222; e-mail: toplice@net.yu; www.hotelroyal.co.yu

Rates: 1/1 23 EUR, 1/2 32 EUR, 1/3 45 EUR. Tax: included in the price. Breakfast: continental, included in the price. Daily accomodation is offered at affordable price.

Cards: Visa, Master Card, Diners Club, EuroCard, DinaCard.

Facilities: restaurant, café, lift, exchange office, room service 24 hours a day, Internet. Rooms: TV, air-conditioning.

SLAVIJA LUX ★★★★

Situated on Slavija square, 1km from the city centre and the Central railway station. "Panorama" Restaurant on the seventh floor has a beautiful view over the city. Good service.

Svetog Save 2; Tel: 2421-120, Fax: 3442-931; e-mail: slavija_hotels@jat.com; www.slavija-hotel.com

Rates: 1/1 105 EUR, 1/2 140 EUR, App 175-200 EUR. Tax: not included in the price (100 dinars/day); Breakfast: buffet, included in the price.

Cards: Diners Club, Visa, Master Card, Maestro.

Facilities: restaurants, piano bar, exchange office, casino, garage (paid separately), fitness centre, lift, room service, wake-up service. Rooms: air-conditioning, TV in room, mini bar, hair-dryer.

ZLATNIK *****

Small, luxury hotel. Situated in a quite street in Zemun, 7km from the city centre. Built as an extension of the famous restaurant, with one of the best cuisines in town.

Slavonska 26; Tel: 3167-511, Fax: 3167-235;
e-mail office@hotelzlatnik.com; www.hotelzlatnik.com

Rates: 1/1 120 EUR, 1/2 146 EUR, APP 160-295 EUR. Tax: not included in the price. (100 dinars/day). Breakfast: buffet, included in the price.

Cards: Diners Club, Visa, Master Card.

Facilities: 2 restaurants, conference hall (up to 40 seats), business centre, gift shop, cocktail lounge, lift, wake-up service, room service, laundry and dry-cleaning service, connected rooms, non-smokers' rooms, car park, garage (paid separately). Rooms: air-conditioning, cable TV, Internet access, safe box, mini bar, hair-dryer.

Information on all hotels in the city:

Information centres of Tourist Organisation of Belgrade (TOB)
www.tob.co.yu
www.yellowcab.co.yu
www.hotels.co.yu

➔ *More information on making phone calls on page 111.*
➔ *Recommended hotels are marked on our map of Belgrade.*

At the time the guide was witten 1 euro was worth 87 dinars.

Board and lodging:

VILA MARIJA

Near the motorway and the outer city centre, it is situated in a peaceful street, surrounded mainly with family houses. The best private accomodation in town. Comfortable and well equipped rooms. Warm, domestic atmosphere.

Debarska 12; Tel: 2448-484;
e-mail: vilabgd@vila-marijabgd.com;
www.vila-marijabgd.com

Rate: 80 EUR. Tax: included in the price.
Breakfast: buffet, included in the price.

Facilities: car park; a salon, a well equipped kitchen and a terrace for barbecueing in summer; 10 double rooms with bathrooms, cable TV, air-conditioning, mini bar, fridge and a telephone.

Hostels:

OPEN BELGRADE

In the street above the "Sillicone Valley" (see page 80) in wider city centre. Two large supermarkets in the vicinity.

Gospodar Jovanova 42; Tel: 064/2588-754, 064/1505-233;
e-mail: openbelgrade@gmail.com;
www.openbelgrade.com

Rate: 11 EUR. Nine beds, shared bathroom.

STUDENTS' RESIDENCE
(*STUDENTSKI GRAD*)

Open only during summer holidays (1 July - 30 September).

Tošin bunar 143-151 (in New Belgrade, half an hour by bus from the city centre);

Tel: 699-302, 3611-375, Fax: 673-266;
e-mail: studentskigrad@yahoo.com

Rate: 11 EUR. Breakfast: included in the price.

Rooms have 2 or 3 beds and each one has got a bathroom, telephone and a mini-kitchen. Washing and ironing of the clothes is paid separately.

KRALJ ALEKSANDAR I

Open only during summer holidays (1 July - 30 September).

Bulevar Kralja Aleksandra 75 (near the Central railway station and Vukov spomenik);

Tel: 401-800, 3400-440, Fax: 401-536;
e-mail: kraljaleksandarhostel@yahoo.com

Price: 11 EUR. Breakfast: included in the price.

Rooms have 2, 3 or 4 beds and each one has got a bathroom, telephone and a mini-kitchen. Washing and ironing of the clothes is paid separately. The accommodation is on the level of a 3 star hotel.

TIS

A new hostel, not far from the outer city centre. It has 11 rooms with up to 6 beds each. The backyard is convenient for barbecuing. Reservations advisable (by e-mail or telephone) at least a day before the arrival. There is an age limit for the guests (18-42 years of age). Transfer from the airport is possible.

Koste Abrasevića 17; Tel: 3806-050, 2419-434; www.tishostel.co.yu

Rate: 15-20 EUR; Tax: included in the price. Breakfast: included in the price.

Cards: Visa, Master Card, Maestro (2.5% commission)

Facilities: reception 24 hours a day, luggage room, lockers, laundry, car park. Rooms: cable TV, Internet, air-conditioning.

STUDENTS' RESIDENCE "JELICA MILOVANOVIĆ

Open only during school holidays: 22 December - 13 January; 1 May - 7 May; 22 June - 31 August.

Krunska 8 (wider city centre);
Tel: 3248-550, 3220-762.

The restaurant is open only to groups (lunch 3 EUR, dinner 2.5 EUR, lunch packet 2 EUR)

Rates: a couple of categories (rooms with a bathroom) 9-11 EUR (for groups over 20 persons 7.5 EUR), lower category (shared bathroom) 7 EUR (for groups over 20 people 6 EUR).

Facilities: room with a PC, library, fitness studio, indoor basketball court.

MOTEL "LIPOVIČKA ŠUMA"

It is not a printing error. This is a motel, but it is cheap and it is situated on the main road towards Zlatibor and Guča. Open all year round. Good side to this motel is that it is situated in a lovely ambient and it is very cheap. Bad side is that, if you haven't got a car, it will take you an hour to reach the city centre, changing two buses on the way (one of which runs once every hour, the stop is outside the motel), or half an hour by taxi (which is expensive because of the great distance).

Lipovica, 17km from Belgrade; Tel: 8302-184, Fax: 8302-134

Rates: 11-15 EUR for bed and breakfast (bungalows in the forest); 6-8 EUR daily (8am - 7pm)

Facilities: restaurant, car park, café-bar. There is a horse-farm in the vicinity with a riding school. Horse-riding through the forest, particularly on snow in winter, is an unforgettable experience. Horse-riding is about 6 EUR/hour.

Information on hostels:

Belgrade Youth Holiday Association, Makedonska 22/II, Tel: 3231-268, Fax: 3220-762.

www.belgradehostels.com

www.hostels.org.yu

➜ *More information on making phone calls on page 111.*
➜ *Recommended hostels are marked on our map of Belgrade.*

Campsites:
DUNAV **

Batajnički put bb, Zemun (12km from the city centre). Tel: 3160-477, fax 610-425; e-mail: amkjedinstvo@ptt.yu

Rates: bungalow 1/2 11 EUR, camp 1 EUR, automobile 1 EUR, bus 4 EUR, motorcycle 1 EUR, connection to electricity supplies: 1.5 EUR. Tax: not included in the price (100 dinars/day). Breakfast: not included in the price. Cards: not accepted.

Motels:
ŠARIĆ

Famous for its lamb and pork roast.

Ibarski put 6 (Ibarska magistrala, 15km from Belgrade). Tel: 8325-419, Fax: 8325-420.

Rates: 1/1 33 EUR, 1/2 45 EUR. Tax: included in the price. Breakfast: included in the price.

Cards: Diners Club, Visa, Master Card, DinaCard.

Facilities: restaurant, car park, exchange office, wake-up service, room service. Rooms: air-conditioning, TV, mini bar, hair-dryer.

Interesting places

Interesting places

Belgrade is, like all large cities, covered by various kinds of garbage, but most of all by the unbelieveable number of billboards. When staying in Belgrade, or looking at the photographs in this guide, you will notice that the sky above the city is crisscrossed by various wires and cables. Not even the citizens know what the great part of those wires are for : have they captured Belgrade stopping its progress, or do they keep it firmly together?

The face of Belgrade is also marked with scars from past wars. The city was completely destroyed 40 times and that is why you will not see a building more than 250 years old, although it is one of the oldest cities in Europe. Many architects and city planners competed with the conquerors in destroying the city. Still, here and there, you can find some beautiful houses which miraculously managed to avoid fire, bombs and man s stupidity. They keep the memories and the smells of the past in their hallways. Here are some interesting places in the city where you will surely feel the spirit of the past and the joy of the present.

Belgrade Fortress and Kalemegdan Park

Belgrade Fortress was erected on the ridge above the Sava-Danube confluence at the end of the 1st century (Roman castrum was the permanent camp of IV Flavius Legion). In the course of history it has been expanded, destroyed, rebuilt and modified.

Before we continue describing the fortress we will mention some of the more important events in the history of the city.

7000 BC - First Neolithic settlement.

600 BC- Thracian and Scythian tribes inhabit the region.

279 BC - The name of the city, Singidunum, is mentioned for the first time. It is inhabited by the Celtic tribe of Scordiscs.

91. AD - Singidunum is inhabited by the Romans. IV Flavi's Legion resides there. Some time later, a Roman emperor is born in Singidunum: Claudius Flavius Iovianus. The first bridge connecting two banks of the Sava.

Baked clay lid. Culture of Vinča, V millennium BC

395. - The Roman Empire is divided into the Eastern and the Western. Singidunum becomes part of the Eastern Empire and its position on the border between the two empires determines its destiny (different cultural influences are mixed, and the greatest number of battles in history will be fought for it due to its important, strategic position).

Bronze Scythian pendant, 5th century BC

441. - The Huns conquer Singidunum.

450. - The Sarmatians conquer Singidunum.

470. - The Goths conquer Singidunum.

488. - The Gepidians conquer Singidunum.

504. - The Goths conquer Singidunum.

510. - The Byzantine Empire gets Singidunum through peaceful agreement.

535. - The Byzantine emperor Justinian I rebuilds the city.

584. - The Avars conquer Singidunum.

592. - Byzantium takes over the rule of the city once again.

630. - The Slavs conquer Singidunum.

827. - The Bulgarians get Singidunum.

878. - Slavic name of the city, Belgrade, is mentioned for the first time in writing (it is mentioned in the letter in which Pope John VIII informs Prince Boris-Mihail of Bulgaria that he dismissed the Belgrade episcope for lechery).

896. - Hungary attacks Belgrade.

971. - Byzantium conquers Belgrade.

976. - Macedonian emperor Samuilo gets Belgrade.

Baked clay statuette. Culture of Vinča, IV millennium BC

1018. - Byzantium gets Belgrade.

1096. - Hungarian army destroys Belgrade but it stays under the Byzantine rule.

1096. - (and 1147) Armies of Crusaders pass through Belgrade (some of them plunder it, too).

1127. - Hungarian army destroys Belgrade and uses that stone to build Zemun Fortress.

1154. - Byzantine army destroys Zemun and brings back that stone over the river to rebuild Belgrade Fortress.

1182. - Hungary conquers Belgrade.

1185. - Byzantium takes over Belgrade through diplomatic negotiations.

1189. - Friedrich Barbarosa passes through Belgrade leading the crusade.

1230. - Bulgaria takes over Belgrade.

1232. - Hungary takes over Belgrade.

1284. - Serbian king Stefan Dragutin takes over Belgrade. The city is in Serbian hands for the first time.

1316. - King Stefan Milutin burns down the city in the war against his brother Dragutin.

1319. - Hungary imposes its rule over the city once more.

1403. - Despot Stefan Lazarević gets Belgrade from Hungary and rebuilds it, making it the first Serbian capital.

1427. - Hungary takes over Belgrade after the death of Despot Stefan Lazarević.

Gold coins of Emperor Constantine I (306-337)

1440. - Turkey attacks Belgrade. Sultan Murat II besieges the city with 100,000 soldiers and 200 ships. He builds fort Žrnov on mount Avala in order to control the access roads to the city. The Turks try to enter the city through underground tunnels but the people from Belgrade mine them and succeed in defending themselves.

1456. - Sultan Mehmed II besieges the city with 150,000 soldiers. The Christian army defending the city is led by Janos Hunyadi and Abbot Giovanni da Capestrano. After difficult battles and wounding of the Sultan, the Turks give up the siege.

1521. - Sultan Suleiman the Magnificent conquers Belgrade with 300,000 soldiers, captures all citizens and transports them to Istanbul by force. The way to Western Europe and Vienna is free. Belgrade becomes the centre of the Ottoman fleet.

Prince Miloš Obrenović (1780-1860)

Belgrade in the late 17th century

1688. - Habsburg army conquers Belgrade in a counter-coup after defending Vienna. All of them meticulously plunder the city, the Turks on their way out and the Austrians on their way in.

1690. - Turkey conquers Belgrade.

1717. - Austrian army (100,000 soldiers) under the command of Eugene of Savoy beats the Turks (200,000 soldiers) and conquers Belgrade. The Austrians rebuild and expand Belgrade Fortress using the most modern system in those times and it becomes one of the largest in Europe. The city progresses a great deal in a short period. The house in which Eugene of Savoy stayed (in those times it was a tavern "At the White Bear") still stands in Zemun.

1739. - Turkey takes over Belgrade through peaceful agreement. The newly-built fortress is taken down and the Turks start building their own from scratch.

1789. - Austrian army, under the command of Feld-

King Petar I Karađorđević (1844-1921)

marschal Laudon conquers Belgrade.

1791. - Turkey besieges and takes over Belgrade through peaceful agreement.

1801. - Rebel janizary (elite Turkish soldiers – most often kidnapped Christian children) take Belgrade Fortress and start terrorising the citizens. This culminates in "killing of the princes" (assassination of the most eminent Serbs). The Serbs answer with an uprising led by Đorđe Petrović - Karađorđe in 1804.

1806. - Under the leadership of Karađorđe, the Serbs free the city, and in 1807 they free the fortress as well. Belgrade becomes the capital of Serbia. The government is in session in the city and the predecessor of the University, "Velika škola", opens.

1811. - Karađorđe is chosen for a hereditary sovereign.

1813. - Turkey conquers Belgrade. The uprising is over. Karađorđe leaves for Austria and later for Russia.

1815. - Miloš Obrenović leads the Second Serbian Uprising. Serbian-Turkish duality of government begins.

1817. - Traditional internal conflicts among the Serbs continue. Karađorđe is killed upon returning to Serbia by order of Miloš Obrenović.

1830. - Sultan's Hatisherif on the autonomy of Serbia. Miloš Obrenović is recognised as a hereditary prince.

1840. - First post office opened in Belgrade.

1844. - National museum founded.

1862. - Conflict on Čukur-fountain (Turkish soldiers seriously wounded a Serbian boy, the Serbs reacted to that, and the Turks shelld the city from the fortress). The conflict ended in international agreement by which the Turks did not have authority over the city any more.

1867. - The Turks leave Belgrade. Turkish commander gives Prince Mihailo Obrenović the keys to Belgrade Fortress where

King Aleksandar Karađorđević (1888-1934)

the Turkish flag remains as the sole symbol of Ottoman rule.

1876. - Serbian-Turkish war. Turkish flag is taken down from Belgrade Fortress.

1878. - Independence of Serbia confirmed at the congress in Berlin.

1882. - Serbia becomes a kingdom, and Prince Mihailo Obrenović the first King.

1883. - First telephone lines are introduced.

1893. - Electrical lighting installed, and in 1894 first route of electric tram becomes operational.

1903. - The May takeover. Group of officers called the "Black hand" kills King Aleksandar Obrenović and Queen Draga Mašin (they thought the King should not have married for love a considerably older woman of common background who could not give him an

Procession of captured Turkish soldiers through the streets of Belgrade in 1912

Celebration on 30 January 1921 when Belgrade recieved the Legion of Honour

heir). Obrenović dynasty is finished, King Petar I Karađorđević comes to the throne (grandson to Karađorđe, finished the Military Academy in Saint-Cyr, decorated with the Order of the Legion of Honour for his merits in the Foreign Legion). He triumphs with the Serbian army in the Balkan wars against Turkey (1912) and Bulgaria (1913).

1914. - King Petar I transfers the authority to the heir to the throne Aleksandar because of his poor health. First World War starts. The Austrians shelld and conquer Belgrade. After the victories on Cer Mt. and the Kolubara Rv,

Englishwoman Flora Sanders, the only female officer in the Serbian army during the First World War. Decorated with Karađorđe's Star.

and the defeat of the Austrian army, the Serbian army frees Belgrade.

1915. - Germany and Bulgaria join the war. German and Austrian troups, under the command of Feldmarschal Mackensen, conquer Belgrade. A three-year occupation and a

Celebration of the opening to traffic of the suspension bridge dedicated to King Aleksandar, 16 December 1934

systematic plundering of the city begin.

1918. - Serbian army returns to Belgrade which becomes the capital of the Kingdom of Serbs, Croats and Slovenes.

1920. - French Marshal and Honorary Duke of Serbian army Franchet d'Esperey decorates Belgrade with the Order of the Legion of Honour.

1929. - Radio Belgrade starts broadcasting.

1934. - King Aleksandar assassinated in Marseille, while he was trying to strengthen a defensive union with France against Germany. The bridge "Chivalrous King Aleksandar" is built over the Sava (destroyed in the Second World War).

1935. - Pančevački bridge constructed.

1939. - Grand Prix race driven around Kalemegdan (forerunner of the present Formula 1).

1941. - 27 March, demonstrations against accepting the Tripartite Pact (Germany-Italy-Japan) that lead to

*Car races around
Kalemegdan in 1939*

the change of government.
The heir to the throne Petar
is pronounced of age and
takes over the rule. The
Germans bombard Bel-
grade on 6 April (many
people are killed, wild
beasts from the Zoo which
survived the bombing roam
the streets of the city) and
occupy it on 12 April. The
king and the government
leave the country. Some
Belgrade citizens are hang-
ed on the lamp-posts on
Terazije and some are
shot down in Jajinci below
Avala. Two Serbian resistance movements are formed
- Tito's partisans and chet-
nicks of Draža Mihailović.

1944. - Americans bombard Belgrade in April, at
Easter, and a couple of
more times in the course
of the same year (many
Belgrade citizens are killed). Tito's partisans and
Red Army free the city on
20 October, new govern-
ment arrests and shoots
many citizens.

1945. - Monarchy is abolished, Socialist Federal
Republic of Yugoslavia is
formed and the rule of
Josip Broz Tito begins.
Belgrade is rebuilt in the
post-war years and be-
comes an important inter-
national political, sports
and cultural centre.
The heir to the throne
Aleksandar, son of King
Petar II is born in Claridge's,
the hotel in London (its
suite 212 is pronounced
for Yugoslav territory).
His godparents were King

*King Petar II Karađorđević
with Field Marshal Mont-
gomery and Prime Minister
Winston Churchill*

*The building of the post office near
the railway station destroyed in
bombing, together with a number
of other beautiful buildings*

Tito and a cheetah

*The building of the
General Staff after the
NATO bombing in 1999*

George and Princess
Elizabeth (now Queen
Elizabeth II).

1961. - First conference of
nonaligned countries is
held.

1968. - Student protests
against social differences
and bureaucracy.

1980. - Tito dies. Officials
from 125 countries gather
at his funeral.

1991. - Unsolved national
and political problems
lead to disintegration of
Yugoslavia. For the first
time in his life, the heir to
the throne Aleksandar II
comes to Belgrade.

1992. - Federal Republic of
Yugoslavia is proclaimed.
United Nations Security
Council imposes econom-
ic sanctions on it.

1993. - The greatest inflation in the history of
humankind.
A 500,000,000,000 dinar
bill is issued in Belgrade.

1994. - The end of inflation, new dinar is intro-
duced.

1996. - Civil protest for non-
acknowledgement of the
results on local elections.

1999. - NATO airplanes
bombard Belgrade for
three months (in April
the Americans and the
Germans finally succeed
in bombing the city to-
gether). Thanks to the
President of France the
bridges in Belgrade are
spared.

2000. - Civil protests for
cheating on general elec-
tions. Federal Parliament
building demolished.

2002. - Federal Republic of
Yugoslavia changes its
concept and becomes the
State Union of Serbia and
Montenegro.

2003. - Serbian Prime
Minister Dr Zoran Đinđić
assassinated in Belgrade.

The complex of Belgrade Fortress comprises Upper town, Lower town and Kalemegdan Park. The present shape of the walls was formed at the end of the 18th century, although the greatest part of the buildings was destroyed in the wars led from those times to the present.

Kalemegdan Park

It was cultivated at the end of the 19th century on an empty plateau in front of Belgrade Fortress which served for spotting the enemy when he approached. The greenery was planted between 1873 and 1875. There are numerous sculptures, music pavillions, Art Pavillion "Cvijeta Zuzorić", the Zoo, children's amusement park. It is a favourite meeting place of chess players, squirrels and couples in love.

Gratitude to France Monument

The monument was erected in 1930 as a sign of gratitude to France for the help given in the First World War. The author is Ivan Meštrović.

The Zoo

Founded in 1936, today it is known as "The Garden of Good Hope". Owing to the efforts of the manager Vuk Bojović and staff it is an excellent spot for all animal-lovers. Special attraction for children is the Baby Zoo where all wild baby animals born in the Zoo are kept. Open: 8am-8pm, in winter 8am-5pm.

Upper town

Pobednik Monument
(The Victor)

The symbol of Belgrade, 14m high, bronze statue on a stone pillar. Author is Ivan Meštrović. The "Pobednik" was erected in 1928 on the 10th anniversary of the breakthrough of the front near Thessalonica (great victory of the Serbian army in the First World War). It was supposed to be erected on Terazije but due to a great public resistance towards a sculpture of a realistically portrayed male nude standing in the city centre, it was decided that it be placed on the present spot, inside Belgrade Fortress, "facing" Zemun. Amazing sunsets can be seen from the plateau next to the "Pobednik" Monument.

Monument to Despot Stefan Lazarević

It was erected in 1982, the author is Nebojša Mitrić. Despot Stefan Lazarević (1377-1427), warrior and poet, first made Belgrade the capital of all Serbian countries.

He became Prince when he was 12 after his father Prince Lazar was killed in the Battle of Kosovo. Apart from being one of the most educated people of his age (he encouraged the development of architecture and arts), he was also distinguished for his bravery in the battles near Rovin, Nikopolis and Ankara. He was among the most eminent of 24 knights of the Order of the Dragon and received Belgrade as a gift from Hungary.

Despot's Gate

It was erected in the first half of the 15th century and is the best preserved part of the fort from the time of despot Stefan Lazarević (the rest of the castle was destroyed in a great explosion of a dynamite storage at the end of the 17th cen-

tury). For a long time it was the main gate to the Upper town. The tower next to the gate is used as an Astronomical Observatory.

Sahat-Tower
(Clock-tower)

It was erected in the 18th century above the South gate of the Outer town. The Turks used it as an observation post. It is possible to climb the tower (the groups are formed every hour between 10am and 5pm (in summer to 9pm), registering is in the tourist bureau inside the South gate).

Roman Well

A mysterious structure 62m deep (10m below the Sava's riverbed). The Austrians renovated it at the beginning of the 18th century so that the fortress could be better supplied with water. There is a spiral staircase around the well leading down to its bottom. Many have

Zindan-Tower

It was built in the middle of the 15th century and was the best fortified entrance to the fortress. The basement of this edifice served as a dungeon.

Jakšić Tower

It was built in 1460 as the main cannon tower of the fort. It was greately demolished at the beginning of the 18th century, and completely rebuilt in 1937. Today it houses the café "Tvrdava" (Fortress).

Ružica Church

(Rose Church) Temple of the Birth of the Most Holy Virgin

In the 18th century the present church (the first was torn down by the Turks in 1521) was a gunpowder storehouse which was turned into an army church in 1869. The church was damaged in the First World War and renovat-

disappeared in its murky waters (nobody knows where these waters come from) and their bodies haven't been found to this day. It can be visited in the same manner as Sahat-tower.

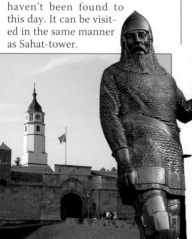

ed in 1925. There are two bronze statues of Serbian warriors at its entrance, one from the Middle Ages and one from the First World War.

St. Petka's Church

The present church was built in 1937 above the miraculous spring (in the Middle Ages there stood a church with the holy relics of St. Petka greatly respected by Belgraders).

Lower town

Comprises the riverbank area of the fortress where the main part of the city was situated in the Middle Ages. It was surrounded by walls and had a fully functioning pier. Only a couple of buildings survived on that spot to this day.

Nebojša Tower

It was built in 1460 as a cannon tower and was one of the docking towers between which an iron chain was spread, closing the entrance to the port. During the Ottoman rule it was turned into a dungeon and a torture chamber, and it was there that the Greek revolutionary and poet Rhigas Pheraids was executed in 1789.

Hammam

A warm Turkish bath – hammam, was built at the end of the 18th century It was restored in 1962 and today it houses the Planetarium of the Astronomic Society "Ruđer Bošković".

1915 Defenders of Belgrade Monument

It is situated on the bank of the Danube, the author is Kolja Milutinović. It was erected in 1988 and it is dedicated to the soldiers who sac-rificed their lives defending the city from the Germans in the First World War. Words from the last order of Major Dragutin Gavrilović, who commanded the defence, are inscribed on the monument:

"At three o'clock sharp the enemy has to be crushed by your violent attack, by your bombs and bayonets. The honour of Belgrade, our capital, has to be saved. Soldiers, heroes, the High Command has deleted our regiment from the list. Our regiment has been sacrificed for the King and Country. You do not have to worry about your non-existent lives any more. Forward to glory! Long live the King! Long live Belgrade!"

Karl VI Gate

It was built in 1736 as a ceremonial entrance to this part of the city and it was dedicated to Emperor Karl VI.

Museums

Although Belgraders are proud of their history, they often treat their historical heritage with indifference. Many valuable exhibits were ruined or stolen because of carelessness and insufficient financial support. The City Museum still does not have its own premises, and the National Museum* has been closed for years due to the inappropriate conditions for exhibitions. The items that a group of enthusiasts managed to preserve were taken by various conquerors. Still, the heritage of this city is so rich that there are a couple of museums that will surely be interesting to you and show you a part of Belgrade and world history. The entrance fee to most places is up to 2 euros. The inscriptions on the exhibits are usually in Serbian and English language.

*The National Museum is situated on Republic Square. It houses the artifacts from these regions from the prehistoric times to the present day. It also possesses a large collection of paintings by foreign painters (especially Impressionists), but the most valuable artifact kept in the museum is **Miroslavljevo jevandelje** (Miroslav's Gospel) - the oldest Cyrillic manuscript (from 1190) with exquisite illustrations. www.narodnimuzej.org.yu

Military Museum

It was founded in 1878. The greatest part of the collection was taken away by the Germans in the Second World War. The items that remained cover the period from the prehistoric times to the present day (weapons, war flags, paintings, photographs, equipment, uniforms, decorations, artillery...). The permanent exhibition is

in the museum building and artillery weapons (18th-20th centuries) and armored vehicles are displayed on the wall and in the trench beside the museum.

Belgrade Fortress; Open: 10am-5pm (in winter to 4pm), Sundays 10am-1pm, Mondays closed.

Aviation Museum

There are various kinds of flying machines, engines, equipment, models and photographs. The exhibits are displayed in the museum building and on the plateau around it. It is widely known for original

Ethnographic Museum

As part of the permanent exhibition there is a very rich collection of national clothes, rugs, craftwork, tools, furniture, old field

and well preserved models of aircraft: Messerchmitt Me-109, Hurricane Mk IV, Spitfire Mk Vc, Yak-3, Illushin IL-2, Thunderbolt P-47... Here you can find the remnants of the only F-117 shot down in the world (in 1999), as well as the remnants of the shot down F-16, cruising missiles and unmanned aircraft.

"Nikola Tesla" Airport (the way to the museum is marked);
Open 8:30am-6:30pm, Monday 8:30am-3:30pm (in winter, from November to April, 9am-2pm, Mondays closed).

→ The same advice is given for getting to the museum as for the transport to the airport on page 10.

photographs... Thematic exhibitions are organised occasionally. In the museum, there is a souvenir

and folk handicrafts shop.
Studentski trg 13; Open: 10am-5pm, Sunday 10am-1pm, Mondays closed; www.etnomuzej.co.yu

Princess Ljubica's Residence
(Konak Kneginje Ljubice)

Representative city house from the first half of the 19th century (finished in 1831), built on commission of Prince Miloš Obrenović for the residence of his family – Princess Ljubica and sons Milan

and Mihailo. Permanent exhibition consists of original furniture comprising various styles from the 19th century Belgrade (classicism, Biedermeier, neo-baroque and oriental styles). In the cellar, in the "Hall under the arches" thematic exhibitions are organised.

Kneza Sime Markovića 8; Open: 10am-5pm, Sunday 10am-1pm, Mondays closed; www.mbg.org.yu

Museum of Nikola Tesla

Nikola Tesla (1856-1943) is one of the most important people for the development of the electricity science. He invented alternating current, three-phase system for elec-

tric energy transfer, induction motor, high-frequency electric current generator and transformer; he was a pioneer in radiotechnics and remote control... Magnetic field unit bears his name. Personal legacy, science papers and the urn with his ashes are kept in the museum. For the visits scheduled in advance demonstrations of some of his experiments are organised.

Krunska 51; Tel: 2433-886; Open: 10am-6pm, Saturday and Sunday 10am-1pm, Mondays closed; www.tesla-museum.org

Automobile Museum

Permanent exhibition is the collection of old cars acquired by Bratislav Petković. The museum

is situated in the rooms of the first public garage dating from 1929. The oldest car in the collection is Marot Gardon from 1897. The museum possesses the collection of old racing motorcycles, photographs, various equipment and a souvenir shop. It is cold in winter since the large space is heated with difficulty. Taking photographs is not allowed.

Majke Jevrosime 30;
Open: 11am-7pm.

Museum of Yugoslav Film Archives

One of the five richest film archives in the world. Apart from the great collection of films, film placards, photographs and scripts, it possesses the original film camera "Lumière" number 335 from 1896. The films from the archive are shown every day in the cinema of the museum (Kosovska 11), and every year, in October, Festival of Nitrite Films is organised. www.kinoteka.org.yu

25th May Museum

The burial place of Josip Broz Tito (1892-1980), the mysterious man who ruled Yugoslavia for 35 years. The leader of one of the two resistance movements, he came into power after the Second World War. President for life and the founder of the Nonaligned Movement. A great charmer and seducer, a hedonist with a refined taste, equally liked by the working class, Hollywood stars, Communist dictators and European aristocracy. Even Churchill, who hated the Communists, came to visit him. The greatest number of statesmen (from 125 countries) gathered at his funeral. In the museum you can see his grave and precious gifts he received from the statesmen and citizens from all over the world.

The location is marked on our map of Belgrade;
Open: 10am-3pm

St. Sava's Temple
(*Hram Svetog Save*)
on Vračar plateau

Preparations for the building of the Temple began in 1894, and the building itself in 1936. It was interrupted by the German attack on Yugoslavia in 1941. The building was continued in 1985 when the state issued the permit. The decoration of the Temple's interior is currently in progress. St. Sava's Temple is the largest votive temple of Serbian people. Its basis measures 91x81m, capacity is 170,000 m3, and it can receive the congregation of 10,000 people. On the central

dome, weighing 4,000t, there is a 12m high gilded cross – the highest point in the city.

Saint Sava
Serbian Archbishop (1169-1236)

Born under the name of Rastko Nemanjić, son of Stefan Nemanja, the Serbian grand prince. He chose spiritual life instead of state power and for that reason ran to Sveta

St. Sava - frescoe from the Mileševa Monastery

Gora, where he was ordained under the name of Sava. He obtained the independence of Serbian Church and became the first Serbian

New building of the National Library

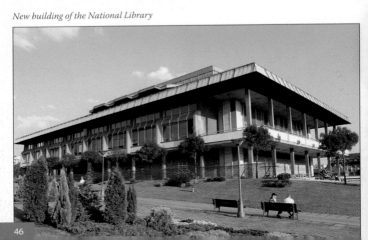

Archbishop. By forming Serbian Church he also formed Serbian state and culture. Together with his father, he erected Hilandar Monastery on Sveta Gora. He reconciled his brothers who fought for power and worked for the benefit of all the peoples in the Balkans. On the order of Sinnan-pasha, the Turks carried his holy relics from Mileševa Monastery to Vračar plateau where they burnt them at the stake in 1594.

On the plateau in front of Saint Sava's Temple there is a monument dedicated to **Karađorđe**, erected in 1979 (the work of Sreten Stojanović) and the new building of the **National Library of Serbia**, opened in 1973 (the old one was situated on Kosančićev venac but burnt down when the Germans bombarded Belgrade together with the complete collection of books and invaluable Cyrillic manuscripts from the Middle Ages).

Đorđe Petrović
the leader of the First Serbian Uprising (1768-1817)

The Turks called him Karađorđe - *Crni Đorđe* (Black George). He was a cattle merchant who fought against the Turks, first as an outlaw and then as a volunteer in the Austro-Turkish war (he recieved the Gold medal for courage). At the beginning of 1804 he was elected the leader of the Serbian uprising against the Turks. He led the battle of Mišar (studied on many military academies in the world) and freed Belgrade in 1806. After the failure of the uprising in 1813 he leaves for Austria and Russia. He was killed upon his return to Serbia in 1817, on the order of Miloš Obrenović. He is the foun-der of Karađorđević dynasty.

Monument to Karadordein front of St. Sava's Temple

Kosančićev venac

It is situated on the high ground above the Sava's pier. Walking on the cobblestones of this street you will feel the spirit of old Belgrade. It was here that the Serbian settlement outside the walls of the fortress was founded during the Middle Ages and started to spread later on. Today, there are art studios and galleries, the office of the President of the Univeristy of Arts and the remnants of the National Library destroyed in German bombing in 1941.

Near Kosančićev venac there is The Orthodox Cathedral (Saborna crkva*) (finished in 1840, dedicated to the Holy Archangel Michael; the relics of the holy Tsar Uroš lie in the church; Vuk Karadžić, Dositej Obradović and the monarchs of the Obrenović

dynasty - Miloš, Mihailo and Milan were buried there, too), Patriarch's Residence of Serbian Orthodox Church (comprising the library and the Museum of Serbian Orthodox Church; the building was finished in 1935, and the number of rooms equals the number of days in the year), Princess Ljubica's Residence, "?" Inn...

*When you are visiting churches and other holy buildings you are expected to behave decently and talk quietly. You can enter the church while the service is in progress but try not to disturb it and not to draw attention to yourself. It is not allowed to enter in shorts, slippers, a mini skirt, with uncovered belly... Women are not allowed to go behind the altar. Taking photographs is allowed with the permission granted beforehand.

The bust of Kosančić Ivan, the medieval Serbian hero the street was named after

Ada Ciganlija

An island on the river Sava, the most visited bathing-place and weekend resort of Belgraders. Artificial lake, 4.2km long, around 200m wide, and 4-6m deep, was created by connecting the island with the mainland by two embankments. There are gravel beaches on both sides of the lake where up to 300,000 Belgraders sunbathe in summer. The beaches are supplied with toilet facilities, catering establishments and equipped for water sports. Swimming season (during

which the rescue team works every day from 10am to 7pm) is from 15 June to the end of September. The water is warm and clean for swimming (although it is muddy so you can't see anything when you are snorkeling). There are several kinds of fishes in it (fishing competitions are organised, the largest carp caught last year had 18kg), and some otters live in the part of the lake where there is no beach. Apart from water sports (swimming, kayaking, rowing, windsurfing, cable for waterskiing) there is a great number of football pitches (it is played 2 halftimes for 15 minutes, the winner stays in), basketball (it is played to 21 points, the winner stays in), and volleyball courts which are all free, all you need is a ball and some friends. On Ada Ciganlija there is also a trim-track, table tennis, tennis courts, bowling alley, artificial climbing wall, bungee jumping platform above the water (55m high), a nine-hole golf-course, minigolf, rugby pitch, paint-ball field, aqua football, simulator in the snowboard centre, grass hockey, skating park. The forest on the

island is crisscrossed with numerous roads suitable for cycling and rollerblading, and you can also see the island from the carriage or a little tourist train that goes around it. There are a number of inns and cafés on the coast of Ada and on the rafts, as well as picnic spots. Apart form other facilites for children, there is a theatre-playground "Robinson's Island".

From the New Belgrade bloks 45 and 70 there is an organised transport by boats to Ada Ciganlija (from 8am to 8pm, return ticket is not more than 1 euro). Cyclists can use the boats, too. On our map of Belgrade we have marked a large car park at the entrance to the island (daily ticket is not more than 1 euro). There is no point in visiting the island by car, unless you are going to one of the restaurant-rafts on the furthest end of the island. In that case, the island is entered by car at the check point marked on our map (entrance ticket is a couple of times more expensive than the usual parking card).

The lake freezes in winter but it is not wise to walk or skate on it since the ice is very thin.

> *The places from which the boat transport to Ada is organised are marked on our map of Belgrade.*

Ada safari

A small lake on Ada Ciganlija covering 6ha. It was stocked with capital carps (the largest number in one place in Europe). Apart from carp, there is grass carp, gibel carp and tench in the lake, too. Fishing permit is paid for, and you can only take a picture with your catch which is then returned to the lake. The lake is situated in the centenary woods, and there is also the "Opušteno" Restaurant where the non-fishermen can enjoy pork roast. www.adasafari.co.yu

The boat for the transport across the Sava

Gardoš

Old ambience-complex in Zemun, a very romantic place. Small and narrow streets with colourful houses

where the summer silence is disturbed only by the chirping of swallows. There is a great number of small

towers were erected on the borders of the Empire, and this in Zemun is the South one. The remnants of Zemun Fortress, dating from the 15th century, are scattered around the Tower.

inns and fish restaurants with great ambience. Millennium Tower built by Austria-Hungary in 1896 to celebrate the 1000th anniversary of the Empire, dominates Gardoš. Four identical

Royal Compound

The Royal Compound, covering the area of 135ha, is situated on top of Dedinje Hill, today the most exclusive residential area in the city. King Aleksandar I personally invested in the building of the Royal Palace (built in 1929) and White Palace (built in 1937, for the use of his sons) with ancillary buildings. On tour of the Royal Compound (the details are on page 116) you can see representative rooms in both palaces, art objects and paintings (Poussin, Breugel, Canaletto, Veronese, Rembrandt, etc.), Palace Chapel, Palace park and the grave of Davorjanka Paunović, the secretary and the greatest love of Josip Broz Tito (He abolished the monarchy when he came to po-

wer and moved to the Royal Compound).

From 2001 the Royal Compound is again the residence of the Royal Family of Serbia and Yugoslavia,

HRH Heir to the throne Aleksandar Karađorđević (first on the left) with his guests at his sixtieth birthday celebration

HRH Heir to the throne Aleksandar II Karađorđević, Princess Katarina, Princes Petar, Filip and Aleksandar.

www.kraljevina.org

Topčider and Košutnjak

In the valley of the river Topčider there is Topčider Park, a beutiful place to spend a sunny afternoon in. Miloš Obrenović* started culltivating it in 1831 by building the residence, church, army barracks and the inn. The residence was finished in 1834 and it was there that

the Prince spent the last years of his rule and died. When the building was over, a plane-tree was planted

in the lime hole, next to the residence, and it is now protected as a natural rarity. It is 44m high, its crown measures 50m in radius and it casts a shade of over 1,400 m2. You can get a ride through the park in the carriage and have lamb roast or sea fish for lunch in the garden of the "Milošev konak" Restaurant (Miloš's Residence). There is a monument to doctor Archibald Reiss (1876-1930), erected in the honour of this Swiss professor, publicist and criminologist, who came to Serbia as the member of the Board for identifying war crimes of Austrian and Bulgarian occupying forces, and stayed in Belgrade for life, founding the technical service of Belgrade police.

*Miloš Obrenović (1780-1860), the

leader of the Second Serbian Uprising and the Prince of Serbia. The founder of Obrenović dynasty.

Košutnjak is a park-forest, covering the area of 330ha (deciduous and evergreen trees) and situated on a 250m high hill. It was open to public in 1903, until then it was a closed royal hunting ground. There are numerous paths and trim-tracks going through the woods, and covered tables with benches for the picnickers are placed on the clearings. Sports-recreational centre Košutnjak has got five outdoor and one indoor swimming pool, football pitches, tennis, volleyball and basketball courts. The shadows cast by the trees hide a couple of restaurants, and there is a spring called "Hajdučka česma" (Haiduks' Foun-tain) at the foot of the hill (drinking water). If you see some cars hidden away in the bushes by the side of the road – just give them a wide berth; they didn't skid off the road, and they don't need your help.

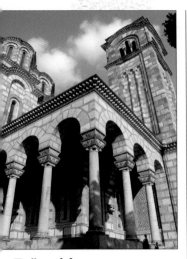

hence the name) are situated here.

Underground rooms, which formed when blocks of stone were taken out, had various usages over time: as food storages, military storehouses and shelters during the wars. During the Second World War the German Command for South-Eastern Europe was placed here (it was General Alexander von Lohr's shelter in an emergency). All these underground rooms and a natural cave can be visited (details on page 116).

St. Mark's Church

It was built from 1931 to 1940 in Serbian-Byzantine style next to the old church dating back to 1835 (it was burnt down when the Germans bombarded the city in 1941).

Furnishing and decorating of the interior is not finished yet. A very rich collection of Serbian icons and the reliquary of Tsar Dušan is kept in the church.

Tašmajdan

Part of the city at the beginning of Bulevar Kralja Aleksandara. For centuries, since the Roman times, its underground part was used as a quarry (in Turkish tašmajdan means "rock quarry"), and its part above ground as a graveyard. The

graveyard was moved to the present "New Cemetery" at the end of the 19th century. It was on Tašmajdan that Hatisherif was read in 1830 – the proclamation of the Turkish Sultan giving Serbia internal freedom.

St. Mark's Church, Russian Church, outdoor and indoor swimming pools of the sports centre, the building of the national television (bombarded in 1999), Central post office (built in 1934), children's cultural centre and "Duško Radović" Theatre, nice garden of "Madera" Restaurant and "Poslednja šansa" Inn (*The Last Chance* - it used to stay open longer than other inns,

Russian Church

The church was built in 1924 by the Russian immigrants and General Vrangel, the last commander of the Russian Royal Guard, is buried here.

Terazije

The centre of the city and the Balkan Peninsula. All distances are measured from here. Terazije is

his rule after his father's death in 1860 and was killed while walking in Košutnjak in 1868. There is a variety of representative buildings and civil houses built at the end of the 19th century.

dominated by "Albanija" Palace, finished in 1940, the tallest building in Belgrade for many years. The mammoth skeleton was found when the foundations were dug. It was named after the inn which used to be on that spot. Terazije fountain, the work of Franz Lorain, was placed there in 1860.

Republic Square
(*Trg Republike*)

The main city square where the buildings of the National Theatre, National Museum and Monument to Prince Mihailo (erected in 1882, the work of Enrico Pazzi) are situated – the popular meeting-place of Belgraders. The infamous Stambol Gate, the main entrance to Belgrade Fortress, was once situated here.

Knez Mihailova Street

The city's central promenade and commercial zone. For pedestrians only. It bears the name of Prince Mihailo Obrenović, the younger son of Prince Miloš. He started

Antique fair in Skadarlija

Skadarlija

Belgrade ambience-complex dating from the end of the 19th century. It comprises Skadarska Street where the famous Belgrade inns ("Dva jele-

na", "Tri šešira", "Dva bela goluba", "Zlatni bokal", "Ima dana", "Skadarlija"), galleries, antique and souvenir shops are situated. At the beginning of the 20th century it became the meeting-place of Belgrade's art life, a bohemian place where writers, journalists, painters and actors gather.

If You Have Some More Time Left...

Parliament

The building was started in 1907 and finished in 1936. The interior of the building is richly decorated.

Parliament. Finished in 1884. It was seriously damaged in both World Wars. The architecture of the palace was greatly changed when it was reconstructed after the Second World War. Up to 1944 Pionir Park was an enclosed palace garden. There is an observation post of the High Command of the Serbian army transported from the front at Thessalonica (First World War).

The sculpture composition "Black Horses at Play", the work of Toma Rosandić, was set in front of the main entrance in 1939.

Old Palace and Pionir Park

The Old Palace is a former palace of Obrenović dynasty, today the City

Botanical Garden "Jevremovac"

Ideal place to have a rest in during sightseeing. A number of different species of plants from all over the world cover the area of 5ha. One part of it was turned into the Japanese garden. It is open from 9am to 7pm, the entry fee is symbolical.

often changed shape due to the torrents of the capricious Danube, and it got the present shape in 1944, when two German barges were sunk by running onto some underwater mines; the Danube sand drifts covered them and the main current changed direction.

Underground train station "Vukov spomenik" (Monument to Vuk)

This station is interesting because Belgrade has got the deepest underground train station in Europe (43m deep) although it does not have an underground. The escalators leading to it are 65m long and 7.5m wide.

Great War Island
(*Veliko ratno ostrvo*)

It is situated on the very confluence of the Sava and the Danube. Its name comes from being an important strategic point for conquering or defending the city. Rare and endangered bird species settled here and it is an ideal spot for birdwatching. There is a sandbank on the upper corner of the island – the Lido beach. In summer there is an organised boat transport or a pontoon bridge from Zemun quay. Through the history the island has

Avala

A mountain (just about – 511m high) in the vicinity of Belgrade. It is an extinct volcano covered by deciduous and evergreen trees. There is a mausoleum at the top – The Monument to the Unknown Hero (work of Ivan Meštrović), erected in 1938, dedicated to Serbian soldiers killed in the First World War. The renovation of the television tower, demolished in the bombing in 1999, is in progress.

→ The locations of all places mentioned are marked on our map of Belgrade.

Food and drink

National Cuisine

The cuisine reflects the historical circumstances Serbia was in. Authentic ethnic dishes are **kajmak**, **gibanica** and **užička pršuta**. Other Serbian dishes are a mixture of different influences from other cuisines but are prepared in a unique style in Serbia. The food you will find here (in restaurants, shops or Serbian homes) is healthy and completely natural (organic, as it is called in other places). There is no genetically modified food or artificial tastes; cattle and chickens eat food of plant origin. A lot of meat is put in all the dishes and favourite vegetables are cabbage and peppers – the ingredients of the largest number of specialties. Soya is not used in human nutrition. Vegetables are bought fresh, on green markets. There you can also buy the best cheese and kajmak, straight from the peasants.

People in Serbia have always spent the most on food. When something is being celebrated the dishes and sweets are prepared for days in advance – so that nothing is lacking. In the end, very often, a whole pork is roast-

ed, just in case. In summer it is obligatory to go somewhere outside and make a barbecue. While some of the people argue about the best way to bake the meat, the others play football on the plain and women cut vegetables for the salad. You will be surprised to see how Belgraders are slim and well-built in spite of all these specialties. That is because they eat a lot of fresh vegetables (in the form of a salad) and they are physically active. No diet or cereals will help you preserve the ideal weight if you spend time at home being a

couch-potato. Those who came to Belgrade with a backpack, and do not have money to spend in restaurants, will not be denied the taste of Serbian cuisine. Fast food shops are almost on every corner; the portions are large and cost 2 euros on average (150g of grilled meat). The dressings are usually free, only kajmak and urnebes salad are charged. You can take our recommendation for the best quality fast food, but try to manage to go to a restaurant and taste the "slow food", at least once.

Breakfast

Standard breakfast for half of Belgraders is a cigarette and a cup of coffee before going to work. On the way to work they drop by a bakery for **burek** (or "pogačice sa čvarcima" - buns with greaves) and yoghurt. Burek is a type of multilayered grease pie with minced meat. It is of Turkish origin but the one in Belgrade is made in a special style and the taste is completely different from the Turkish original. Burek is made in round baking dishes, it is cut in triangular pieces at your wish (ask for 250g, for a start) and apart from meat, it can be filled with cheese or without any filling. It is eaten in the bakery at the table (you will get cutlery) or is taken away.

Cold starters

Every proper lunch starts with a glass of cooled brandy, to increase the appetite and warm the heart. Then cold starters follow, to kill time until the main course arrives. The starters we will mention are often eaten on their own, for breakfast or snack. These are: **proja** (corn bread; cheese or kajmak are frequently added into the pastry), **gibanica** (Serbian pie made from special filo pastry with eggs, cheese and kajmak; it can be eaten cold but it is best when eaten very hot, along with cold sour cream), **prebranac** (large beans cooked with spices and braised onion; served cold), **kajmak** (salty dairy product), **white cheese** (there are various kinds, cow's and sheep cheeses; it is best to try "sjenički"), **užička pršuta** (dry-cured beef or pork prosciutto from Užice), **čvarci** (greaves) (melted lard and some pieces of meat in the form suitable for nibbling; subtype – **duvan čvarci** (tobacco greaves, the name comes from their shape which reminds of tobacco), slice of bread coated with lard and seasoned with salt and paprika, **pihtije** (jelly, winter starter; pig's feet and meat from the head are boiled with spices, garlic and paprika are added next

and then the liquid is poured into shallow containers and cooled until it turns into a jelly). Some of these starters are eaten on their own, and some can be combined. Some of them taste the best when eaten with fingers. Apart from gibanica, there are various other pies: with cheese, dock, leek, pumpkin, potatoes, apples, sour cherries... The best ones are made with hand-made filo pastry.

Gibanica and proja

Warm starters

The most frequently prepared ones are: breaded peppers stuffed with cheese and kajmak, **pita zeljanica** - dock pie (cheese and dock or spinach), **cicvara** (*kačamak* - polenta) prepared in a special way with cottage cheese and kajmak), and in summer, breaded zucchini with tartare sauce (mayonnaise and gherkins). Apart from these, the majority of restaurants serve breaded caciocavallo cheese with tartar sauce and grilled mushrooms as a warm starter.

Soups and pottages

Serbian housewives prepare many different kinds of soups and pot-

tages. We will mention the ones usually served in restaurants and which should not be missed. Those are the veal and lamb pottages, and nettle pottage can be found in a couple of places. The pottages are made with lots of meat and vegetables, they are served hot and a couple of drops of vinegar can be added after serving. On the river, you can try the fish soup which is made of different kinds of freshwater fish and is usually served in small iron pots on the table. There is no single recipe for a fish soup because that is usually a chef's secret and the question of prestige that attracts the customers.

Main courses

They usually consist of meat prepared in various ways and vegetables on the side. We will list the ones most frequently found in Belgrade restaurants.

- **Roštilj** (Grilled meat): various kinds of grilled meat with fine chopped onions on the side. Although many nations prepare meat in this way, Serbs have raised it to the level of art and

these kinds of specialties you won't be able to try anywhere else. The meat is prepared in a special way in order to be grilled over the fire made from beech charcoal only. Grill chefs are a special class of cooks and the best ones are from the town of Leskovac in the South of Serbia. Grilled meat is

divided into: **ćevapi** (minced meat fingers, especially delicious when served on kajmak), **pljeskavice** (round shaped meat of 5 to 10 ćevapi on the "pile"), **kobasice** (sausages - special grill variant, usually a little spicy), **ražnjići** (kebabs - meat cut into little pieces and arranged on a stick), **vešalice** (pork chop without bones, cut lengthwise; they can be white or cured), **pileća džigerica uvijena u slaninu** (chicken liver rolled in bacon), **leskovački uštipci** (minced meat and paprika in the form of little doughnuts), etc. If you order **mešano meso** you will get a piece of all the meat mentioned on one plate. If you order **leskovački voz** (Train from Leskovac) you will get all the meat mentioned on separate plates that will be arriving one after the other, so that each kind of meat is served perfectly warm. The authors of this guide haven't yet heard that anyone managed to eat all the "carriages".

- **Leskovačka mućkalica**: braised pieces of pepper, tomato, onion, paprika and finely cut grilled meat.

- **Karađorđeva šnicla** (Steak Karađorđe): rolled and breaded veal steak stuffed with kajmak, served with tartare sauce. It was named after Karađorđe, the leader of the First Serbian Uprising against the Turks. It is also called "A Girl's Dream".

- **Sarma**: minced meat, rice and spices rolled into sauerkraut leaves.

- **Jagnjeća sarmica**: finely cut lamb liver and lungs, rice, eggs, onions and spices are rolled into lamb's caul, covered with milk and eggs and then baked in an oven. They are served with cold sour cream.

- **Podvarak**: sauerkraut braised on onion and finely cut bacon. It is

Svadbarski kupus simmers on live coals

eaten as a separate dish or served with roast.

- **Svadbarski kupus**: layers of sauerkraut with lamb, veal and pork meat (fresh and cured) cooked in a large earthen pot for several hours, the longer the better.

- **Punjene tikvice**: hollowed young zucchini stuffed with rice and minced lamb and pork. Served with cold sour cream.

- **Čorbast pasulj** (bean soup): if you want to test your stomach. It is cooked with onion, laurel, paprika, bacon and cured ribs and braised in the end.

- **Pečenje** (roast): a standard choice for the ones who can't make up their mind or like simple food. Lamb, pork, and sometimes kid, are spit-roasted over the fire made from beech charcoal. It is so tasty that even the well-mannered ones forget about manners and lick their fingers in the end. The meat is measured by kilos, and you can order as much as you want (a kilo of meat is enough for three men if they're not very hungry). Be sure to try **jagnjetina ispod sača** (lamb roast under sač – an earthen pot with a lid). Pieces of lamb and potatoes are put in sač which is then covered with live coals.

Fish

There is a great number of recipes for preparing fish in all the cuisines around the world, but when the fresh fish is taken out of the river right under your table on one of the raft-restaurants, it is the best when surprised a little in a pan and served right away. You can only overdo it with **pijani** "drunk" (cooked in white wine) or smoked carp. The fish tastes the best when served with Swiss chard or potato salad (cold potato is cut in circles with onion and pepper). Sea fish lovers will not be denied their pleasure since fresh sea fish is almost daily shipped by plane or train from the seaside.

Salads

In Serbia salads are eaten with the main course. Fresh vegetables are eaten in summer and **turšija** and baked peppers in winter. Summer salads are: **Srpska** (Serbian) (tomato, cucumber, pepper, onion, chilli, oil and salt), **Šopska** (the same as Serbian with the addition of grated cheese), **cooked beetroot**, **lettuce** (there can be various kinds of lettuce with the addition of radishes, seasoned with oil and vinegar), **cabbage** (seasoned with oil and vinegar) and **spring onions** in spring.

Turšija is the mixture of pickled peppers, green tomatoes, carrots, cauliflowers and gherkins. **Cabbage** is pickled separately and is served chopped and seasoned with oil and paprika (sweet or hot). **Turšija** and sauerkraut go excellently together with good brandy. **Rasol** (brine, the liquid in which the cabbage was pickled) is drunk as a medicine against hangover. More winter salads: baked pepper (it is baked on live coals or on electric ring, peeled and seasoned with oil, vinegar, salt and garlic – the men who are courting tend to avoid it) and **ajvar** (chutney; baked and peeled pepper and aubergine ground and cooked with spices; subtype is **pinđur** for which the pepper is not ground but chopped and mixed with tomato and little chilies). Every self-respecting lady of the house prepares food provisions for winter (winter salads and jams) by herself and has got "the best" recipe for **ajvar** and **turšija**.

For the ones who like it hot there are fresh chillies, baked chillies with garlic in oil, pickled chillies, **urnebes** salad (paprika with cheese) and horseradish (clears the sinuses). Chopped fresh onion is traditionally served with grilled meat.

Bread

Bread is immediately put on the table and is eaten with all the dishes during the entire lunch. It is common to ask for more bread if you have eaten all that was brought. On the bill it is marked as "cuver" and the price is usually the same, no matter how much you eat. Better restaurants serve a couple of kinds of bread (white, brown, corn, etc.) and various spreads (butter, **urnebes**, cheese spread) to keep you occupied while you are waiting for the main course. The top of restaurant offer is when they knead and bake home-made – **pogača** (pitta bread), by themselves. It is eaten warm with **kajmak**.

Sweets

The sweets usually offered in most of the restaurants are: palačinke (crepes) with various fillings, "sladoled" (ice-cream), "voćni kup" (fruit salads), "torta" (cakes), but if you want to try something characteristic for this city order **orasnice** (walnut sticks), **suva pita sa orasima** (very sweet walnut filo pie), **pita sa višnjama** (cherry filo pie), **salčići** (made from lard, white flour and sugar) and **vanilice** (white flour, walnut, sugar pastry filled with jam). You have probably noticed that walnuts are the favourite ingredient in the sweets made in the inns; men especially like them. You will figure out why. Belgraders do not eat light cakes either; they are usually made of eggs, butter, chocolate, walnuts and hazelnuts.

In the pastry shops you can try **žito** if you haven't been invited to a Serbian "Slava" where it is served. **Žito** is cooked wheat mixed with ground walnuts, sugar, icing sugar, vanilla and nutmeg. It is served cold, optionally topped with whipped cream.

Slatko
(fruit preserves)

"Slatko" is frequently served with coffee. It is the way to preserve the whole fruit for winter. It has a unique taste and is most frequently consumed in the morning before breakfast, or as refreshment when you arrive somewhere since it is an excellent source of energy. One or two teaspoons of "slatko" are taken together with a glass of cold water. "Slatko" is made of wild strawberries, blueberries, wild blackberries, blackcurrants, sour cherries, plums, and, even, rose petals. "Foodland" Company produces "Bakina tajna" (Grandma's Secret), various kinds of "slatko" prepared in the traditional style (fruit, sugar and citric acid boiled on a wood-burning stove).

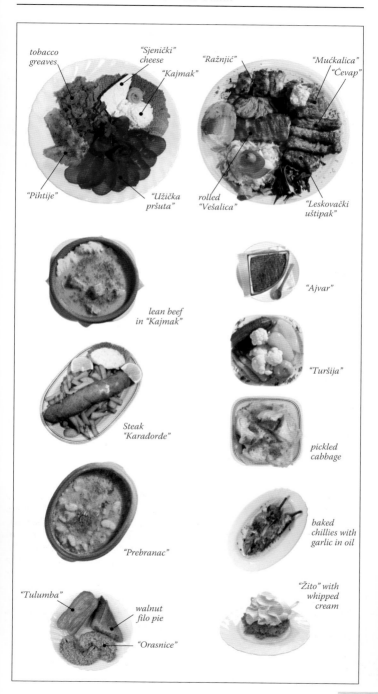

tobacco greaves

"Sjenički" cheese

"Kajmak"

"Ražnjić"

"Mućkalica"

"Ćevap"

"Pihtije"

"Užička pršuta"

rolled "Vešalica"

"Leskovački uštipak"

lean beef in "Kajmak"

"Ajvar"

Steak "Karađorđe"

"Turšija"

pickled cabbage

"Prebranac"

baked chillies with garlic in oil

"Tulumba"

walnut filo pie

"Orasnice"

"Žito" with whipped cream

National Drink

Serbs drink a lot, either to get into a better mood or to repress everyday worries. That is the reason why they prefer natural drinks that don't cause headache in the morning. National drink is **rakija šljivovica** (plum brandy). It is considered to have healing properties and can be for external and internal use. It is made of various kinds of plum, and the best one is made of "požegača" plum. Taste it while you can, since this variety is destroyed by the illness called "šarka" and in a couple of years' time there won't be any more požegača. Every self-respecting village host has got a brandy still and makes his own brandy. Apart from plum, good brandy is made of apricot, grape (called **loza**), pear (called **viljamovka**), quince, apple, honey (called **medovača**), and **travarica**, **komovica** and **kleka** are made when brandy is mixed with medicinal herbs.

How brandy is made

Good brandy is made of ripe and healthy, unsprayed fruit. Unripe, rotten or damaged fruit, as well as the stones, are discarded. Healthy fruit is chopped and put to ferment in a clean barrel which is filled to 80% of its capacity and protected from external influences. When the fermentation is finished the distillation shoud not be postponed. Neighbours and friends are called in to make the

Brandy making in the street in 1935

time spent next to the brandy still shorter through conversation and tasting. The middle part of the distillate, containing around 30% of alcohol, is used for the brandy. That "soft" brandy is put into the clean brandy still again and the process is repeated. Still, only the middle part of the distillate is separated, so that around 30 litres of strong brandy are produced from 100 litres of "soft" one. The distillation process is called "brandy baking" in Serbia, and the double distilled brandy is called "**prepečenica**"

("overbaked" brandy). The brandy is "baked" slowly, on a low fire, so that it would not get burned. A good brandy contains 40-45% of al

cohol, it slides down the throat, warms the stomach and doesn't burn the mouth.

Before consumption, the brandy is stored in glass containers for 2 months (for the impatient ones) or in oak barrels for a couple of years (for the hedonists). It is served cooled to cellar temperature, in small glasses or **čokanj** (small glass bottle for brandy). It is drunk before or after the meal (in other words, the whole day through), but moderately, because if you overdo it you will not be able to enjoy the smell of fruit.

If you want to take brandy as a souvenir, we recommend **Žuta osa**, **Stara sokolova rakija** and **Zlatna biserka**. Be careful to buy home-made brandy only on recommendation. The price is around 10 euros for a litre.

> *Honey brandy in amphora or earthen carboy coated with beeswax and natural honey in baked clay pots: 063-227-069; www.medeko.co.yu*

Coffee

Domestic coffee and espresso are served in restaurants and cafés. You will order traditional coffee if

you ask for "domaća" (domestic), "turska" (Turkish) (named after the Turks who brought coffee to this area, but it is different from the real Turkish one) or "obična" (regular). It is a strong, black coffee, with lots of froth. It is taken with, or without, sugar. In order to make good coffee, it is necessary that džezva (coffee pot) is never washed with detergent, only rinsed with water. Coffee drinking is a real ritual, an occasion for a conversation and meeting with friends. When you come to somebody's home, it is the first thing that you will be offered. There is a custom for the women living next door to invite each other for a cup of coffee because they snatch at every opportunity to gossip and exchange recipes. When they drink it, they turn the cups upside-down and wait for the coffee grounds to make lines on them. Then, they try to read coffee grounds to each other. Most often, they see a road, money and a soldier.

Other drinks

Serbia has a long tradition of making wine. Try white wines "Krokan", "Smederevka", Chardonnay (Radovanović Litlle Cellar), "Trijumf" (Aleksandrović Wine Cellar), as well as "Varijanta" (rosé) of the same manufacturer. Red wine "Carigrad" (Radenković Wine Cellar) has got an interesting bouquet. The ones who spend a lot of time in the inns like to drink **špricer** (*spritzer*) – white wine with soda. It is good for digestion and doesn't go to the head quickly.

We recommend these domestic varieties of beer: Weifert, Jelen or stout MB. Next Premium juices are excellent (especially raspberry), but DMB are even better (any sort – blackberry, blueberry, raspberry, strawberry) but also harder to find. Bottled slightly-mineralised water brands are Prolom and Rosa.

Recommended Restaurants

A national restaurant in Serbia is called **kafana** (inn). Apart from the basic function as a catering establishment (the consumption of food and drink), the inns are used as places for getting information, making business deals and emotional discharge (nobody goes to a therapist). The most frequent causes for arguments in the inn are politics or paying the bill. Belgraders do not have the custom of sharing the bill, instead, everyone insists on picking up the tab. In certain situations, those discussions can turn into fights. If you happen to witness that kind of incident, stay calm, because the ones who have been fighting a moment ago quickly make peace, burst into tears and kiss each other on the lips. Every Belgrader has

his own favourite inn, or more of them. The first inn in Belgrade (and in Europe) opened on Dorćol in the late 16th century.

City officials sometimes try to surpass various conquerers in distroying the historical heritage. "Tri lista duvana"

Inn (*Three Tobacco Leaves*), where the first telephone in the city rang, was torn down in order to make space for a prefabricated garage, and "Zlatna Moruna" Inn (*Golden Beluga*), where the plot for the assassination of Austro-Hungarian heir to the throne Franz Ferdinand was hatched (which was the cause of the First World War), is a sports betting shop. Some of the good old inns were closed because the new owners are in industrial catering, and a similar fate probably awaits some others.

The menus are in both Serbian and English, and the waiters have a rather good command of English. The portions are generous and only the extremely hungry ones manage to eat up everything. During Lent it is com-

mon to ask the waiter for your meal to be prepared in a certain manner. Smoking is allowed everywhere and there are no separate smokers' rooms. Most of the restaurants have got a fine selection of wines from all over the world. For an aperitif it is best to order brandy (good restaurants frequently offer domestic ones, ask the waiter to recommend it to you). The price of the main course is from 3 to 10 euros, and a complete lunch for one person (soup, main course, salad, dessert and drink) is from 10 to 15 euros. Belgrade waiters are famous for their informal conduct and good memory. If you come to a place more than twice, they will know what your favourite drink is and how much you tip.

Reservations are not necessary but are advisable if you are in a larger

one hour before closing time. Good atmosphere and guests who don't know where their home is prolong the opening hours of some restaurants, sometimes deep into the night. The list of recommended restaurants consists of the restaurants (inns) which deserve to be on it due to the quality of the food served, ambience and service. In other words, the best ones. There is a great number of restaurants spe-

group and want to make sure you get a good place. There are no dress codes. There is no elitism. In the same place you can see people of various social status and education, diplomats, actors and artisans. They do not bother each other because the most important thing is enjoying good food. Opening hours are usually from 8am to 11pm or from noon to 1am. The kitchen is usually open to

cialised in other countries' cuisines in Belgrade, but we did not want to describe them here. You can get the information about these and other restaurants in Belgrade from the kind Belgraders.

List of recommended restaurants:

(In alphabetical order; opening hours are not strict, they can be longer; In brackets you will find more or less literal translations of names of restaurants, songs and clubs because their meaning is often very important)

National and international cuisine

"?"

An old Serbian inn bearing an unusual name situated in one of the oldest houses in the city (built in 1823, has been working as an inn since 1826; the first pool table was put here in 1834). Authentic ambience, traditional cuisine, pleasant staff. In one corner there is a wood-burning stove where beans are cooked and potatoes baked.

Kralja Petra 6; Tel: 635-421; Open: 7am-midnight (Sundays 9am-10pm); Live music in the evening; Garden.

Dačo

Checkered tablecloths, unpaired cutlery, and rustic ambience. Try the rustic hors-d'oeuvre, svadbarski kupus and house wine.

Patrisa Lumumbe 49 (Karaburma); Tel: 2781-009; Open: noon-midnight, Mondays closed; Souvenir shop; Garden (cats and chickens wander between the tables).

Daka

Pleasant ambience, excellent service and beautiful garden in the city centre, isolated from the noises of the city. Try "mućkalica" from three kinds of meat.

Đure Daničića 4; Tel: 3222-068; Open: 11am-1am; Garden.

Dva Jelena (Two Deer)

It was opened in 1867 on the spot of a former bakery. The capacity of seating 1000 diners in 7 rooms of different sizes and ambience. Margaret Thatcher came here a couple of times. For breakfast try "pogačice sa čvarcima" and white wine or sour peppers stuffed with beans. For lunch or dinner try lamb cooked in milk or "papazjanija" (everything with everything else).

Skadarska 32 (Skadarlija); Tel: 3234-885; Open 11am-1am; Live music; Garden.

Đorđe

A top restaurant, excellent food; Try "ribić u kajmaku" (lean beef in kajmak) and honey brandy. Good selection of wines.

Šekspirova 29; Tel: 2660-684; Open: noon-midnight; Live music (piano); Garden; Car park.

Franš

An elegant restaurant named after the French General Franchet d'Espe-rey. Try Steak Karađorđe or "Čudesni tanjir za dve osobe" (A miraculous dish for two). Excellent selection of wines (430 sorts from all parts of the world) and specialties with white and black truffles. A great number of artistic paintings are in the possession of the restaurant and hang on its walls.

Bulevar Oslobođenja 18a; Tel: 2641-944; Open: 9am-1am, Sundays closed; Garden; Car park.

Ima dana (There Are Days...)

A newer inn, opened in 1968 in the house of the fa-mous actor and bohemian Uncle Ilija Stanojević. It is famous for rich snacks, meze (food for picking that goes with drink and conversation). Pelé, Spanish King Juán Carlos, Larry Bird, etc. used to come here.

Skadarska 38 (Skadarlija); Tel: 3234-422; Open: 11am-1am; Live music, perfomances with actors; Garden.

Kalemegdanska terasa
(Kalemegdan Terrace)

Excellent food and selec-tion of wines, beautiful view over the Sava-Danube confluence (two terraces). Try "leskovačka mućkalica."

Kalemegdan; Tel: 3283-011; Open: noon-1am; Live music in the evening; Garden.

Klub književnika
(Writer's Club)

Legendary restaurant in a plain basement of the club; meeting place of politicians, intellectuals and artists. There is no music (not even from the radio) in order not to in-terfere with the discussions. Sophia Loren, Jean Paul Sartre, Hitchcock and others used to come here. Quiet and secluded garden. Food and drink are mainly on waiter's recommen-dation (none of them has less than 20 years of service, and everything is kept under control by the famous Buda - 61 years of service). Try "jagnjeće sarme u maramici" (lamb meat balls in caul) and "krempita" (vanilla slice; a sweet with filo pastry and custard).

Francuska 7; Tel: 2627-931; Open: 8pm-2am, Sundays closed; Garden.

Pastuv (The Stallion)

Watching horse-races on Sunday from the restaurant (reservation needed), while eating "jagnjetina ispod sača" and drinking cold beer, is an unforgettable experience. The waiters are slow, so order everything you want at once.

Racecourse (Hipodrom); Tel: 3548-058; Open: 10am-11pm; Garden; Car park.

Pink

Outside the city centre, so you will need to take a taxi. People from the neighbourhood gather here; relaxed atmosphere, good food, large portions, extremely cheap. Try "leskovački uštipci" and Czech draught beer.

Solunskih boraca 16 (Žarkovo); Tel: 502-091; Open: 10am-midnight; Garden.

Rubin (Ruby)

Isolated in the woods. Excellent grill (they dry-cure the pork chops and make sausages by themselves), Czech beer and view over the city. On Fridays they cook bean soup with dry-cured ribs. For some reason a great number of singing birds gather around this inn so it is a pleasure to take a stroll outside after lunch.

Kneza Višeslava 29 (Košutnjak); Tel: 3512-123; Open: 11am-11pm; Garden; Car park.

Srpska kafana (Serbian Inn)

Another legendary place, opened in 1936. The actors from the neighbouring theatre are regular customers. Try "rolovana piletina sa suvim šljivama" (rolled chicken with figs) or "teleća glava u škembetu" (calf's head in entrails) if you are open for new experiences. Service is a bit slower because the waiters like to sit with the guests, too.

Svetogorska 25; Tel: 3247-197; Open: 10am-midnight; Live music in the evening.

Tabor (Camp)

Legendary restaurant, favourite with Belgraders. Try piquant potatoes, "čačanski uštipci" (meat doughnuts from Čačak) and quince brandy. One of the best bands in the city plays every evening from 8.30pm to 1am. They know everything.

Bulevar Kralja Aleksandra 348 (on the corner with Gospodara Vučića Street); Tel: 2412-464; Open: 10am-1am, Sundays closed; Car park; Live music in the evening.

Zlatnik (Gold Coin)

National and fish restaurant in "Zlatnik" Hotel. Ideal for business lunches. The best beefsteak in town, excellent service and selection of wines.

Slavonska 26 (Zemun); Tel: 3166-256; Open: 6am-11pm; Car park.

Fish restaurants:

(In alphabetical order)

Bevanda (Watered Wine)

Fresh sea fish (not frozen) and sea food prepared in Dalmatian style. Home atmosphere and excellent service (the waiters like to discuss life problems with their guests). If you are hungry, and have enough money, ask for everything in due order (salted anchovies with the apperitive, cold salad, inkfish and white risotto, stewed savory clams, and in the end, choose some fresh fish, sole or gilthead, and finish it off with a surmullet). They have oysters, too.

Požarevačka 51 (on Vračar); Tel: 2447-446; Open: noon-midnight; on Sundays but not on public holidays.

Konoba kod Goce i Renata
(Goca and Renato's Tavern)

It is most beautiful in summer. A couple of tables are on the platform above the water where the fishermen dock and bring fresh fish which is prepared right away. There are only river fish and salads on the menu. Try fish soup, pike, chard and wash it all down with cold Smederevka. The best orasnice in town.

The bank of the Danube on the other side of the river, to the right from Pančevački bridge (the instruction on how to get there is given on our map of Belgrade); Tel: 063-7747-791; Open: 10am-midnight; Car park.

Renato and Goca with the biggest European catfish caught in front of restaurant

Langouste

Very expensive restaurant with Mediterranean cuisine and a fantastic view over the Sava-Danube confluence. The specialty of the house is lobster, of course. Excellent selection of wines.

Kosančićev venac 29; Tel: 3283-680; Open: noon-midnight; Live music (piano); Garden; Car park.

Tramontana

Pleasant atmosphere of a family house with a garden on Banovo brdo. In summer the meals are eaten under candlelight in the garden covered with vine,

and in winter in front of the fireplace, listening to the pleasant crackling of the fire. Fantastic food. Try salmon in white sauce and sea bass prepared in the royal style.

Kraljice Katarine 26; Tel: 3542-237; Open: noon-midnight; Garden.

Pastry shops

Mali princ (Little Prince)

Large selection of pastries and cakes, excellent lemonade. They also make cakes to order. Try "Čežnja".
Braće Nedić 7 and "Mercator" Shopping Centre in New Belgrade; Tel: 2447-934; Open: 9am-9pm.

Mamma's biscuit House & Max House

Something between a pastry shop and a café. Large selection of pastries and cakes, and they have sandwiches, too. Try "Ana" or chocolate tart.
MBH: Strahinjića Bana 72a (Tel: 3283-805); MH: Terazije 40 (Tel: 3620-280); Open: 9am-23pm.

Moskva

Large selection of pastries and cakes in a pastry shop with a long tradition and a view of Terazije. They make cakes to order. Try "Moskva šnit".
"Moskva" Hotel on Terazije; Tel: 2686-255; Open: 8am-11pm.

Panta Rei

About ten kinds of cakes (served in very large slices), ice-creams, fruit salads and a view of the Danube.
Sports Centre "Milan Gale Muškatirović", Danube quay on Dorćol; Open: 9am-1am.

Petković

Home-made cookies and the best "žito" with whipped-cream in town. It was open in 1903. Tel: 3238-730; Ilije Garašanina 4; Open: 9am-9pm.

Poslastičarnica (Pastry shop)

In Brankova and Prizrenska Streets there are two pastry shops where you can try "home-made" sweets (šampite, krempite, tulumbe, various cookies, srneća leda, etc.), "žito" with whipped-cream and different-flavoured varieties of ice-cream. One is called "Poslastičarnica", and the other "Poslastičarnica Specijal". Open: 8am-midnight.

Fast food (In alphabetical order)

Chickenita

Chicken done in various styles. Large portions, great selection of additional dressings, inconvenient for parking. Specialty: stuffed chicken drumsticks.

Makenzijeva 85; Open: daily; Telephone for orders (10am-2am): 2458-279

Čobanov odmor (Peasant's Repose)

Traditional Serbian fast food in authentic ambience. Don't miss this! Lamb and veal pottages, pitta bread with "duvan čvarci" and "kajmak", rolled pork and lamb roast packed for takeaway. Specialty: "čobanska komplet lepinja" (shepherd's full pitta bread; dry-cured ham, kajmak and dripping).

Vojvode Šupljikca 34 (on Vračar); Open: daily; Telephone for orders (10am-midnight, minimum 5 euros): 2450-947

Gvero

The best fast grill in town. It has got a place for sitting, too. You have to wait a couple of minutes. Specialty: "small pljeskavica", made of 5 "ćevap" (200g of meat, there is a larger one made of 10 "ćevap").

Corner of Omladinskih brigada and Milutina Milankovića Streets; Open: 8am-10.30pm, Sundays closed. Tel: 2163-135

Ipanema

Excellent restaurant with Mediterranean specialties. There is a "counter" on the street functioning separately where you can buy Italian sandwiches, pasta, tiramisu and profiteroles packed for takeaway. Specialty: sandwich in walnut bread and tiramisu.

Strahinjića Bana 68; Restaurant is open from 9am to 1am (Sundays to noon), and the counter with fast food from 9am until everything made that day is sold, you can try to 8pm.

Loki

Legendary fast food place, named after the owner's dog. If you saw someone in the disco and couldn't come up to her, "Loki" is your second chance because many people finish their night out right here. First you order, then wait in line to be called when your order is ready. The store is divided into two identical kiosks, you can order in either of them. Specialty of the house: chicken drumsticks.

Corner of Kralja Petra and Gospodar Jovanova Streets; Open: daily

Pekara (Bakery)

There are many quality bakeries in the city that prepare burek and pastries in traditional style. You will find them on your own (if they are not selling slices of pizza and cans of coke, you're on the right spot) or with the help of Belgraders. We would like to point out the one in the oldest preserved house in the city (built in 1727), in 10 Cara Dušana Street on Dorćol (which is the oldest part of the city apart from Belgrade Fortress. In Turkish the name translates as "four way crossroads".) There were seven houses like that in a line, but this is the only one still standing after various bombings and conquests of Belgrade.

→ More information on making phone calls on page111.
→ The recommended restaurants are marked on our map of Belgrade.

Night life

Night life

Night-life is one of the things that has made Belgrade famous and it probably leaves the strongest impression on first-time visitors to the city. The reasons for that are the spirit of Belgraders and positive atmosphere that make you feel as if you are at your friend's home.

The Habits of Belgraders

Actually, the night-life in Belgrade starts during the day when people psychologically prepare themselves by sitting in one of the numerous cafés. That can turn into an arduous and long-lasting activity, in jargon known as chilling out or "blejanje" (literally "bleating") (in summer lying in the sun and in winter sitting by the window of a café, for a long period of time). The best chill out spots are: any of the cafés on Obilićev venac (during the day girls gather here to exchange experiences after strenuous shopping and to gossip about the passers-by because these cafés have an excellent view of the ex-

its from the surrounding shopping centres), any of the cafés in Strahinjića Bana Street* (known as the "Silicon valley" or the "Aquarium", since the term for a girl, in Belgrade jargon, is "riba" - fish), any of the cafés in Njegoševa Street, near Cvetni trg, or the cafés: "Bre", "Monument", "Street" where the relaxed atmosphere attracts the girls who like reading books.

One of Belgrade's secrets that mysti-

fies foreign visitors is the fact that every day, during working hours, most of the cafés are packed. In scientific circles this problem equals the one regarding the existence of the tenth planet, because physics claims that one entity (an employed Belgrader or a student) cannot be in two places at the same time, in addition to the aggravating circumstance of the difficult economic situation in our country.

People go out spontaneously, without much planning, at any hour, regardless of the job that awaits them the next day. Cafés are open until 1am or 2am, and clubs until 4am or 5am. People go out every day of the week – the best fun and the largest crowd do not de-

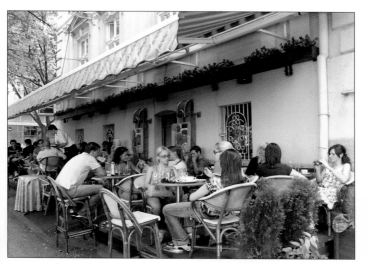

pend on the day of the week but on the circumstances. Depending on the type of fun you prefer a night out can start around 8pm (with a visit to the theatre or dinner), or around 11pm with a drink in a café, and then continue with a wild party on one of the rafts till it's time for the morning burek to recover strength with the first rays of the morning sun. The entrance to the majority of the clubs is free and if it is payed, it is not more than 5 euros. You are not obliged to wear a tie anywhere, although you will not be allowed to enter some places wearing trainers.

If you come early (before midnight) to a club or a disco, you will probably get the impression that you have come to a literary evening. Nobody is dancing; people are eyeing each other and trying to look disinterested, as if they are bored since they came there "by chance". Main topics of conversation are Tao of Physics, constitutional rights or Kubrick's Aesthetics. If you are patient enough and wait for the moment which is difficult to pinpoint, and even more difficult to predict, everything around you will turn upside-down. When Belgraders hear the song they really like they dance on the tables in a burst of wonderful energy, and girls who have looked at you deprecatingly just a moment ago will throw themselves into your arms.

The rafts are a specific segment of Belgrade night-life. There are about a hundred of them and they vary in shape, capacity and music that is played. They are isolated, far away from the residential areas, and because of that the party can go on all night if the guests are in the right mood. The boats are interesting, too. At the beginning of the evening passengers, food and musicians board the boats and then they cruise down the rivers around the city while the

and in some unusual places from time to time. Belgrade clubs make a

stock of fuel and good mood lasts.**
Concerts, guest performances by famous DJs and parties for special purposes are held all year round in "Sava" Centre, Youth Cultural Centre (Dom omladine), Student Cultural Centre (SKC), Belgrade arena, KPGT,

* If you want to get to know Serbs a little better, find someone to tell you stories about people that Belgrade streets were named after. Strahinjića Bana Street was named after the medieval Serbian hero (he is also known as Banović Strahinja), celebrated in folk epic poems (Goethe studied Serbian in order to read them in the original). His story goes like this: while Strahinja was visiting his father-in-law, Vlah Alija the Turk separated from the main part of the army which was preparing to attack Serbia, set fire to Strahinja's estate, killed his mother and abducted his wife. On hearing this, Strahinja asked his father-in-law Jug Bogdan and his sons – the nine Jugović brothers, to accompany him in the rescue of his wife. They refused to go and get killed by the Turks in vain since she was already dishonoured. Led by love, Banović Strahinja went alone to get her, across the Turkish land, dressed as a Turk. His wife, who didn't take the kidnapping to heart and even started enjoying it, recognised her husband and warned Vlah Alija. The two of them started fighting, all day till noon. When his wife saw that they coud not overpower one another, she took Banović Strahinja's sword and hit her husband on the head, because she liked the Turk better now. However, the wound was not deep enough and Banović Strahinja got more strength from it. He slit the Turk's throat with his teeth, and then started to weep for killing a better man than himself. He took his wife home and forgave her because he loved her and because he did not have anyone to drink dark red wine with, in his lonely house. He was killed (as well as his father-in-law and all brothers-in-law) on Kosovo in 1389 in the battle between Serbian and Turkish armies.

break from June to the beginning of October. The parties move to the rivers and open spaces. All self-respecting cafés and restaurants set up their gardens, which are open to the end of October. Clubs and cafés on Ada Ciganlija start working. Most of them

Every regime changed the names of some streets of its own accord. The names currently in use are shown in the guide and on the map.

have deckchairs on the beach, perfect for taking a nap in the sun, or mustering strength for the night party. In

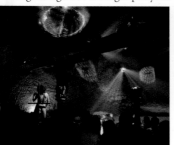

the evening, candles and torches are lit in the gardens, and blankets are there for you in case of cold weather. Beach volleyball courts next to the cafés are lit and rented by the hour, along with a ball. Some of the cafés are open throughout the year. Warning: lifeguards are not on duty

at night, so if you swim while under the influence of alcohol, you can be in danger.

The best partying is usually in some small, hidden places which we won't disclose here, because they would lose in quality if the word gets around. You will discover them yourself if you explore Belgrade patiently enough, or Belgraders will take you there themselves, if they decide you deserve it.

** When you go to the river at night it is wise to take a thin sweater because it always gets chilly near the river. It is good to have a mosquito repellent also since swarms of these bloodsuckers start appearing at sunset and attack viciously for a couple of hours.

Mr Stefan Brown, Wednesday, around 5am

National Music

Serbia has a very rich music tradition and a number of various styles of folk music can be heard in Belgrade. The favourite spots are those with live music, no matter whether those are jazz, blues or rock clubs or inns with folk music. There are various types of bands: old town (guitar, violin, bass), tamburitza (tamburitza, guitar, bass), "folk" (accordion, violin, clarinette, bass, drum), brass (trumpets, bass, drum)...

In the inns where the musicians go from table to table, play "to the ear" to the guests and fulfill their wishes, it is a custom to pay the band. The time that the band spends at a table is proportional to the amount of money given. It is a special experience to listen to Gypsy bands, whether brass or tamburitza. Gypsies know how to play everything (from Frank Sinatra to authentic old Serbian music), they play everywhere and under all weather conditions, to alleviate their melancholy and rejoice. Gypsy musicians are usually self-taught and they do not play the trumpets – they actually talk through them.

Naturally, Serbs behave irrationally when they listen to music also. They are very emotional (although they don't look like that) and they are willing to leave the whole salary in the inn for a woman. Some of them honestly think that it is better to spend money on the band than on

the food. Sometimes, they make the band play on the table, under the table or "on the TV set" (this means that the band goes outside and plays at the open window). For these kinds of stunts the musicians are generously rewarded – the guests shove

the money down their trumpets, string it on their guitars or stick it to their sweaty foreheads. In any case, it is highly unlikely not to have a good time in Belgrade.

Some nice songs that you can order from the musicians in the inns:

lively - Marš na Drinu (March to the Drina), Donesi vina krčmarice (Landlady, Bring More Wine), Oj Jelo Jelena (Oh, Jela, Jelena), Šešir moj (My Hat), Moja mala nema mane (My Baby Doesn't Have a Fault), Evo banke cigane moj (Here Is a Coin For You My Gypsy), Još litar jedan (One More Litre), Kad je deda lumpovao (When Grandpa Was Merry), Reših da se ženim (I Decided to Marry a Girl), Kad sam bio mlađan lovac ja (When I Was a Young Hunter), U ranu zoru (At the Break of Dawn);

slow - Nizamski rastanak (Nizam's Parting), Svilen konac (Silk Thread), Fijaker star (Old Carriage), Sinoć kad je pao mrak (When the Night Fell Yesterday), Bolujem ja (I Am Ill), Tiho noći (Quiet Night), Kad bi ove ruže male (If These Small Roses Would...), Tamo daleko (There, Far Away), Ima dana (There Are Days...), 'Ajde Kato 'ajde zlato (Come on Kate, Come on Honey), Na te mislim (I'm Thinking of You), Vranjanka (Girl from Vranje), Mito bekrijo (Mita, you debauchee);

a special one (glasses fly by themselves on the very first lines) – Šta će mi život bez tebe dragi (I don't Need Life Without You Darling).

Recommended Café-bars (In alphabetical order)

Amsterdam

The most beautiful garden on the water attracts the most beautiful girls in the city. They offer light food and pastries, in the evening there is usually live music.

Danube quay near "Jugoslavija" Hotel; Tel: 3194-971; Open: 10am-4am

Ben Akiba

A coktail bar. During the day they have sandwiches and pasta and you can treat yourself to one of the books from the shelves. After 9pm funk and new jazz music is played and it is difficult to find a seat at the bar.

The apartment on the first floor in 8, Nušićeva Street (the entrance from the passage), there is a doorbell; Tel: 3237-775; Open: noon-2am

Bollywood

A cocktail bar decorated in Indian style. During the day you can lie on the divan while sipping your drink, but in the evening it is difficult to even stand because of the crowd. 350 different cocktails, 20 varieties of tea.

Šafarikova 11; Tel: 3224-733; Open: 10am-2am (Sundays noon-2am). Garden with sofas.

Crveni rak (Red Crab)

An ale-house, one bitter and four kinds of lager draught. Good selection of domestic brandies. Mainly blues and rock music. After a second round in the evening you will sometimes get snacks for free ("proja", pie, etc).

Beogradska 14 (near Zemun quay and green market); Tel: 064-1833-884; Open: 10am-2am

Galerija

The most romantic café in town with a breathtaking view of the Danube. If a girl has successfully resisted your courting, she will surely "give in" here. They offer food, too.

Čunarska 1 (on Gardoš in Zemun); Tel: 612-096; Open: 10am-1am

Grinet

The place with a widest selection of coffees in town. Try "moka". The coffees can be taken out in the heat-preserving container.

Nušićeva 2; Tel: 3238-474; Open: 8am-midnight

Idiot

A cosy little place where mostly young artists and unusual people gather. In summer people even stand outside the café, holding their drink. In winter you can enjoy excellent choice of music in a small basement.

Dalmatinska 13; Open: noon-2am

Klub svetskih putnika (Association of World Travellers)

An unusual spot in the basement of a residential building. Home atmosphere, a cat on the stove, books about faraway countries and sandwiches on offer during the day.

Bulevar Despota Stefana 7; Tel: 3242-303; Open: 1pm-midnight

Kuglaš (Bowler)

A small café in the place of an old bowling alley (you can bowl in your own clothes and shoes). The favourite spot of rockers and bikers. Rock and blues musicians perform frequently in the evenings. You can eat there if it is an emergency (they don't have a regular "menu" but they've got one pan and if somebody is hungry, they prepare the things they find in the fridge).

Đušina 5; Tel: 3240-324; Open: 10am-4am

Kuća čaja (House of Tea)

A tea-house where you can buy different kinds of tea from China, Japan and Sri Lanka, English and Russian blends, as well as tea sets.

Mileševska 47 (Vračar); Tel: 3445-412; Open: 9am-11pm

Monument

A café in the hammam (Turkish bath) of Prince Miloš Obrenović. Ideal for business meetings. Try excellent salads and Oplenac wine.

Admirala Geprata 14;
Tel: 3617-254;
Open: 10am-1am

Plato (Plateau)

Bookstore, Internet café, restaurant and club with live music (mainly jazz and latino) in one place. Summer garden is famous for its deckchairs, although there is a section with regular chairs, too.

Plateau near Kapetan Miša's Foundation (*Kapetan Mišino zdanje*), between Vasina and Knez Mihailova Streets; Tel: 2635-010; Open: 9am-2am

Street

Ideal for reading a newspaper while having a cup of coffee during daytime, and hanging out with friendly people while listening to good music at night-time.

Dositejeva 19;
Open: 10am-1am

Stara kuća VioletA*

An old house with a restaurant in the basement, a café on the ground-floor, a salon to relax in and a room for intimate dinners on the first floor. Beautiful garden, good cuisine and excellent service.

Topolska 4 (Vračar); Tel: 2431-458; Open: 10am-1am

¿Que Passa?

An elegant café on the ground-floor of "Aleksandar" Hotel. A large selection of domestic and imported drinks, South-American cuisine. Thursday, Friday and Saturday night – live latino music.

Kralja Petra 13-15; Tel: 3305-300; Open: 10-01h

*Old House VioletA - The story about how this inn got its name: A few years ago an old Belgrader, who lived in France between the two World Wars, came up to the owners of the house, while it was being renovated, and asked them to name it Violeta. Right at the beginning of the Second World War in Nancy he met Violette Artaud, a twenty-year old girl from Luneville who worked at the bar of a small bistro. He fell in love with her for her chastity, well-manners and a shy smile. In 89 years he had never seen anything more beautiful and he was afraid that he would not find anything so beautiful in Heaven either, unless he met her again. However, he feared that encounter because Violette had gone there as a nurse and he was afraid to find her with someone younger, gone to Heaven too early, like her. But never mind, he would forgive her, who would have waited for so long? He didn't, either. He got married, had great-grandsons already. He lived a happy life but not a day passed that he had not thought of Violette, although he had not even kissed her. He just held her frozen hands one morning before she volunteered to go to an army hospital. He asked the owners of the inn to name it Violette since he could not have dedicated anything to her because of his wife. He asked them because maybe one day a love like that would happen to them and it would make them eagerly wait for that ferryman to take them to the other bank of the river, and he wouldn't be coming... (he swore). They fulfilled his wish and that is how this inn got the name dadicated to all happy and unhappy loves.

Recommended Clubs and Discos

Akademija

A cult Belgrade club. It was one of the top ten clubs in Europe in the 1980s. It is situated in the dark basement of the Faculty of Fine Arts, and divided into a large and a small club, with different kinds of music each. The DJ is in a metal cage, there are pinball machines in the corners, and beer is consummated mainly. Domestic and foreign alternative rock bends perform here. The entrance fee is not more than 2-3 euros.

Rajićeva 10; Tel: 2627-846; Open: 10pm-4am; www.akademija.net

Andergraund

The best-known disco in town is situated in one of the old caves under the fortress. House, R&B, hip-hop. Be sure not to miss the nights when DJ Puki and DJ Pepe play funk in the small "VIP" lounge. It is a café during the day. The entrance fee is not more than 5 euros. There are two more clubs in underground Belgrade in the vicinity - Sargon and Balthazar.

Belgrade Fortress, the entrance at the crossroads of Pariska and Karađordeva Streets; Tel: 063-407-070; Open: 10am-4am

Barutana (Gunpowder Storehouse)

The club is situated in the former gunpowder storehouse of Belgrade Fortress. Bar-stools and speakers are arranged around sarcophagi and tombstones from the Roman period. Barutana is among the top ten most attractive clubs in Europe on the list of famous European DJs.

Belgrade Fortress, the location is marked on our map of Belgrade; **Open occasionally**.

Crni panteri (Black Panthers)

The best place in town for those who like merry Gypsy musicians. Not for the reserved ones. Cevapi and dzindzi-mindzi are the dishes we strongly recommend. Advance booking required for Fridays, Saturdays, and Sundays.

The location can be found on our map of Belgrade, and taxi drivers know it, too; Tel: 063-369-655;
Open: from sunset until the guests spend the last dinar; Closed Tuesdays; Car park.

Mr Stefan Brown

A view of the city, numerous kinds of cocktails and a great bar in the centre of the club capable of supporting barmen and a bunch of guests dancing on it. Varied programme depending on the day in the week, not for those under 20. It is recommended to arrive earlier (before 01 am) because if it gets too crowded, you may not be allowed to enter.
Business premises on the corner of Sarajevska and Nemanjina Streets, on the ninth floor;
Tel: 065-5566-456;
Open: 10am-4am

Plastik

A modern-style interior mainly with electronic music and frequent guest performances by foreign DJs. Rock bands perform occasionally. A popular spot, the visitors sometimes queue outside.

Corner of Takovska and Dalmatinska Streets;
Tel: 3245-437; Open: 10pm-4am

Ptica - Feeling club (Bird)

The best jazz club in town. It is on two levels and in summer the musicians play in the garden of the club. On Sunday nights people listen to Piazzola and dance tango. There is a store selling rare editions of jazz and classical music, too.
Šantićeva 8; Tel: 3234-614; Open: 10am-2am

Reka (River)

"Reka" is a fish restaurant which found its place on this list because of the excellent atmosphere at night-time. People go there for music and atmosphere (at some weekends the whole inn dances), rather than food. Reservations are advisable.

Kej Oslobođenja 73b (the end of Zemun quay under Gardoš);
Tel: 611-625; Open: 8am-4am

Tramvaj (Tram)

Jazz, blues, funk and latino music. A different band performs each night. Cheap beer, nice people.

Ruzveltova 2 (near the Monument to Vuk);
Tel: 3808-269; Open: 8am-4am

Useful addresses:
www.yellowcab.co.yu
www.izlazak.com
www.chillout.co.yu

→ More information on making phone calls on page 111.

→ *The locations of Belgrade arena, Youth Cultural Centre, Sava Centre, Student Cultural Centre and KPGT are marked on our map of Belgrade. The majority of the rafts are marked on our map of Belgrade. If a raft is marked on the map and you can't find it, it has probably burnt down or sunk.*

Belgrade girls

Belgrade girls are amusing, naughty, dangerous, charming, elusive, witty, conceited, smiling, defiant, cunning, elegant, provocative, unpredictable, proud, cheerful, enigmatic, spoilt, irresistible... Belgrade girls are the soul of this city.

"In order to conquer a city you have to conquer its soul first! "

Danube and Sava

illustrations: Momo Kapor

Traffic

Taxi

Many Belgrade taxi drivers are bad and ruthless drivers. For that reason, we will recommend only three taxi firms (three are about twenty of them). We recommend **Lux taxi** because they have the greatest number of decent and honest drivers, as well as rather good cars. The second firm is Beotaxi which we recommend because they have the greatest number of cars, so when you get into the position that the other firms do not have available cars or do not want to

drive on shorter distances, **Beotaxi** will not let you down. In the end, we recommend **NBA taxi** because their drivers are decent and reliable. The only flaw is that they mainly cover New Belgrade only.

We have already mentioned, at the beginning of this guide, that you should not negotiate the fares in advance since the drivers are obliged to charge the fare that the metre displays. A price list and an identification card of the driver should be visibly displayed in the vehicle. All taxi vehicles need to carry a sign of the firm and the unique sign of the taxi drivers in Belgrade. Transport by taxi is cheaper in Belgrade than in the majority of European countries. The start is about 60 cents, and a kilometer of a ride from 30 to 70 cents (depending on the rate). First rate is on weekdays and Saturdays from 5am to 10pm, second on Sundays, holidays, weekdays and

Saturdays from 10pm to 5am, and the third for the rides outside the city area. The ride from one to the other end of the city does not usually go over 10 euros. The ususal tip is to round the fare to the nearest figure, up to 10%. Transport of personal luggage is included in the fare. If you want a receipt the driver is obliged to issue you one. Pets can be transported by taxi only with the consent of the driver.

You can hail a taxi in the street, ring for it or find it at ranks. Shorter distance ride could pose a problem (e.g. from Terazije to Slavija). If you get rejected for a short distance ride (although it is not by the law), it does not help to argue – better look for another vehicle. Usually the ones who are first at ranks avoid shorter distance rides, but the ones in the rear are disposed for all arrangements.

In Belgrade it is usual to sit next to the taxi driver and make the ride shorter by talking to him. The taxi drivers will be glad to give you information on hotels, restaurants and other things you are interested in. If the taxi driver is smoking and it does not agree wih you, you are free to ask him to put out the cigarette. When you ring for a taxi you can ask for a non-smoker driver.

Lux taxi	Tel: 3033-123
	and 065-3033-123
Beotaxi	Tel: 970
NBA taxi	Tel: 3185-777

→ *More information on making phone calls on page 111.*
→ ***Important ranks are marked on our map of Belgrade.***

Driving a car

If you do not have steady nerves and adventurous spirit it is best to give up driving your own or hired car in Belgrade. Belgraders drive fast and nervously, they change the lane suddenly and without warning and swear at everyone around them because everyone thinks they are right and that they have priority.

If you still decide to drive around Belgrade, pay attention to the following:

- Drive according to regulations and ignore the ones who honk because you did not start immediately on the yellow light or because you are driving at a required speed. Speed limit in town is 60km/h, if not

marked otherwise. In many places in town (especially in the part of the street where the speed limit is 40 or 50km/h) police checks speeding. A child under 12 and a person under the influence of alcohol must not sit on the front seat of the passenger vehicle. Allowed quantity of alcohol in the blood of a driver is 0.05%. The use of belts is obligatory for the driver and a passenger sitting on the seat next to the driver.

- Because of the fact that there are not enough bridges, the bypass still does not exist and the motorway runs almost through the city centre, there are no usual rush-hour times any more – traffic jams are almost always present on all main streets. No one has come up with the explanation, but it is a fact that when it rains the traffic jams and hold-ups are 3-4 times worse than

When you stop at the traffic light some children may approach you and ask for some money or young men offering to wash your car windows. Those are our dear fellow-citizens Romanies (Gypsies), they are cheerful and friendly.

on ordinary days, although the number of vehicles on the streets is not larger. Because of the long driving, and the fall in concentration as well, smaller crashes are common on the bridges Gazela and Brankov, as well as in Bulevar Vojvode Mišića (alongside Belgrade Fair). The only prevention is to keep a safe distance.

- If the right lane in a street is marked with a yellow line, it means that it is reserved for the vehicles of the City transport and taxis. Driving in the yellow lane is fined.

- It is the most comfortable to drive off-road vehicles on the streets of Belgrade because of the great number of holes in the roads. The holes appear mysteriously, even in the recently repaired streets, and they are most dangerous when it rains so they get filled with water and cannot be noticed.

- No matter how relaxed you are,

be prepared to lose your patience when you meet the utility services repairing roads. People in that Belgrade service are convinced that the white colour for the horizontal signalisation on roads lasts longer when it is applied to the road surface in the middle of the worst traffic jam. Apart from that, they believe that when the old layer of tarmac is taken off in a street it is necessary to leave it like that for at least a month. All this, naturally, increases the hold-ups in the traffic.

- However, the greatest danger for the drivers in Belgrade is posed by the attractive and scantily dressed Belgrade girls who walk down the streets. It is worse in summer, although in winter a playful lock of hair above a blue eye can cause damage to the car.

Parking in Belgrade

Parking a car is a problem like in all large cities. Belgrade does not have a sufficient number of public garages, and the majority of business buildings in the centre do not have their own car park. That is the reason why the system of three parking zones was introduced in the old city centre. This is how it works:

At the beginning and the crossroads in every street there is a sign mark-

Registration numbers for Belgrade start with letters "BG"

You will receive the message confirming your payment (if the automatic SMS reply starts with the words: "Zao nam je..." ("We are sorry...") it means that the system is currently out of function and you have to fill in the card). In this way the parking is paid on weekdays from 7am to 9pm and on Saturdays from 7am to 2pm. At other times, you can park your car on the marked spaces without paying for them. Be careful not to leave the car on spaces reserved for the disabled people or firms (clearly marked with a sign), otherwise it will be towed away. If there is a sign "Rezervisano 7-17" underneath the zone sign, it means that the parking

ing the parking zone. Apart from that, the parking spaces on the road are marked with the colour of the corresponding zone. The zones are: red, yellow and green. In the red zone it is allowed to park for one hour for the price of 30 dinars.* After one hour you have to move your car to some other place. The traffic wardens will tolerate a delay up to 15 minutes (not a second more, they are very strict). If you fail to move the car by that time, you will get fined 1,450 dinars* and you have to pay it in the post office (an additional hassle). In the yellow zone it is allowed to park up to 2 hours (price: 25 dinars per hour), and in the green one up to 3 hours (price: 20 dinars per hour). Parking is paid by a parking card for the adequate zone (bought in the newsstands) or by an SMS from your mobile phone. You fill in the cards by crossing out the data that mark the moment when you parked. The next step is to put the card on the dashboard below the windscreen so that the traffic warden can see it. Paying by an SMS works like this: send the plate number of the car (without spaces, e.g. BG308104) to the number of the corresponding zone (9111 for the red, 9112 for the yellow, 9113 for the green zone).

space is reserved for a firm in that period. The traffic wardens fine non-payment of the parking, staying too long in the parking space or invalid payment for the parking (if you made a mistake regarding zone or date).

It is more convenient to leave the car in the public garage because the parking there is not time-limited and you do not have to panic every hour. When you enter the garage take the ticket from the automat next to the ramp. Before driving your car out, you should insert the ticket in the automat for payment (receives the banknotes up to 200 dinars) and then, insert the verified ticket in the automat next to the ramp when leaving the garage.

You can park in the streets that do not belong to any parking zones if there is not a "Zabranjeno parkiranje" (No Parking) sign, if you park at least 5m from the pedestrian crossing or a crossroads and if you do not block a garage.

*At the time the guide was witten 1 euro was worth 87 dinars.

→ Parking zones, public garages, petrol stations open 24 hours a day and places where the illegally parked vehicles are towed away are marked on our map of Belgrade.

Useful telephone numbers and addresses

RENT-A-CAR

Avaco - Trnska 7; Tel: 2433-797, 064-1845-555 (0-24h); avaco@yubc.net; www.avaco.co.yu

AVIS - AUTOTEHNA - Obilićev venac 25, Tel: 2620-362; info@autotehna.com; www.avis.co.yu

Budget - Hotel Hyatt Regency; Tel: 2137-703; office@budget.co.yu; www.budget.co.yu

Hertz - Trg Nikole Pašića 1; Tel: 3346-179; reservation@hertz.co.yu; www.hertz.co.yu

Primero - Bulevar Avnoja 59; Tel: 301-5004; office@primero.co.yu; www.primero.co.yu

VIP - Humska 1; Tel: 3691-890; contact@vip-rentacar.co.yu; www.vip-rentacar.co.yu

Yu Tim - Hotel Jugoslavija; Bulevar Nikole Tesle 3; Tel: 2692-339; yutimrac@eunet.yu; www.yutim.co.yu

JKP "Parking servis" - 27. marta 77; Info media centre (for information on parking and towed away vehicles), Tel: 3035-400; www.parking-servis.co.yu

Service for help and information AMSS (Automobile Association) - Ruzveltova 19-21; Tel: 987 (gives information, technical support on the roads and transport of damaged vehicles). www.amsj.co.yu

"Full-service" car wash, open 24 hours a day: "Petošević" Servis in New Belgrade, marked on our map of Belgrade.

→ Car-repair shops open 24 hours a day have a yellow light flashing on their roofs and they are marked on our map of Belgrade. .

Walking and cycling

The best way to get to know Belgrade, as well as any other city, is on foot, because that is the only way to feel the sounds, smells and atmosphere of a city. The drivers in Belgrade will not hit the pedestrian on purpose but do not expect them to stop the moment you step on the crossing. You have to be brave and insolent on the crossing, the drivers respect that.

Apart from the beautiful female passers-by, the pedestrians should pay attention to the land mines on the pavement left by the dogs. Fines

for irresponsible owners do exist but nobody charges them. The most dangerous zones are Vlajkovićeva, Palmotićeva and Hilandarska Streets, as well as Dorćol, from Vasina to Cara Dušana Street.

There are many stray dogs in Belgrade. They usually go about their business, so if you do not pick on

them they will not pick on you either. In winter, one should be aware of black ice and that would be about all. Belgrade is a very safe city and you can go everywhere on foot, at any time, day or night. Locations of important sights in the city are marked by tourist signposts in English. Watch for open manholes also (sometime the lid is stolen, believe it not).

Cyclists cannot navigate the city easily since thay have to share roads with cars. However, a ride on a bicycle track along the river, from Dorćol to Ada Ciganlija, is a real treat. There are a couple of bike-repair shops along the way. Other

good places for cycling are along the bank of the Sava on New Belgrade side, Zemun quay and Ada Ciganlija. Cycling in Košutnjak and Topčider is not recommended because of steep ascents and the narrow road used by the cars also.

➜ *Bicycle tracks are marked on our map of Belgrade.*

Public City Transport

Although Belgrade has about 2 million citizens and a problem with traffic, it still does not have an undergound, nor will it get one in near future (although it has the deepest underground railway station in

Ticket punching machine

Europe). City transport is carried out by buses, trams and trolley-buses.

The transport by buses is carried out by the municipal service under the jurisdiction of the City Council and a couple of private companies, which means that the buses on the streets come in various shapes, colours and years of manufacture. For all operators (and all kinds of transport) the ticket is the same and it is bought on the news-stands, price: 27 dinars.* The ticket can be bought from the driver immediately on boarding the vehicle. It is more expensive there, 40

dinars.* The tickets should be punched in the machines next to the doors. Transport working hours are, roughly, from 4:30am to 11:30pm. In the night traffic the vehicles run every hour from 12:10am to 2:10am. The ticket for the night transport costs 60 dinars* and it is bought from the driver. In the night traffic

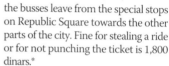

the busses leave from the special stops on Republic Square towards the other parts of the city. Fine for stealing a ride or for not punching the ticket is 1,800 dinars.*

Riding on a tram is a little more exotic since the trams roll like ships on restless seas, and when one of them breaks down – the whole line gets blocked (that, naturally, happens always between the two stops when it is raining).

Public city transport mainly functions

well. It is a quicker mode of transport in the old part of the city than a car since there are special lanes for the buses in most of the streets

*At the time the guide was witten
1 euro was worth 87 dinars.

Useful addresses:
Belgrade City Transport Company,
www.gsp.co.yu
Commuter lines, www.lasta.co.yu

On every stop there is a board with information on city transport lines

Useful information

Opening hours

Banks and post offices are usually open weekdays 8am-5pm, Saturdays 8am-2pm (in "Mercator" Shopping Centre in New Belgrade, the bank is open 9am-9pm, Sundays 9am-5pm).

Exchange offices are open weekdays 8am-8pm, Saturdays 8am-3pm.

Food stores are most often open weekdays 7am-9pm, Saturdays

Meat and Delicates Store* in Vasina Street is open 24 hours a day. "Milan" Butchery in blok 61 in New Belgrade: 7am-10pm (and it grills the meat bought there, specialties – stuffed lamb and stuffed pork). The florist's shop "Lotos", on the corner of Jurija Gagarina and Gandijeva Streets in New Belgrade, is open 24 hours a day (for emergency cases).

You are not likely to find public toilets in Belgrade. There is a decent one (only men's), on the corner of Vasina and Francuska Streets next to the National Theatre and a couple of mixed ones in the public garages. If you have certain needs, you can use the toilets in nearby restaurants and cafés.

*The places mentioned are marked on our map of Belgrade.

7am-6pm (some of them to 9pm), Sundays 7am-3pm (some of them to 5pm). Green markets are open every day 6am-4pm. Shops in the malls are open 10am-8pm (although it is not recommendable to go shopping before 11 o'clock in the morning since many shop-assistants come to work at that time in order not to interrupt their "beauty sleep").

Shopping centres (with supermarkets) "Mercator" and "Super Vero" in New Belgrade are open weekdays and Saturdays 9am-9pm, Sundays 9am-3pm.

In all parts of the city there are small food stores and food stands open 24 hours a day. "Big Bull"

Holidays

Public holidays (pharmacies, shops and institutions on duty are open):

1 and 2 January - New Year

7 January - first day of Orthodox Christmas (no shops are open and there are no people on the streets)

15 February - Serbian Statehood Day

1 and 2 May - Labour Day

Orthodox Easter - from Good Friday to the second day of Easter

Serbian Orthodox Church calculates its Christian religious holi-

days according to the old, Julian calendar, which runs ahead the Gregorian by 14 days. It means that Belgraders use the opportunity to celebrate New Year's Day a couple of times (31 December/1 January – main party; 1 and 2 January – party re-run; 13/14 January – celebration according to Julian calendar).

Electricity

Voltage is 220V, frequency 50 Hz.

Water

Water from the city water su-pply system is chemically and bacteriologically safe, it has an agreeable taste and you can drink it in unlimited quantities.

Tipping

The usual tip is around 10% (it is given in one banknote or by rounding up the amount). Tips are given to waiters, bellboys, parking guards (in front of the restaurants), taxi drivers, hairdressers, people who wash cars (if they do it manually) and mechanics. If you are paying by credit card it is usual to leave the tip in cash. If you are not satisfied with the service, you do not have to give a tip.

Money

Currency exchange is done in all banks, post offices and exchange offices. Serbian official currency is the dinar (CSD). One dinar consists of 100 para. Coins are: 50 para, 1, 2, 5, 10, 20 dinars. Denominations of notes are: 10, 20, 50, 100, 200, 500, 1,000 and 5,000 dinars. Yearly inflation is from 10 to 15%. At the time the guide was written 1 euro was worth 87 dinars.

It is prohibited by law to pay in foreign currencies. Money can be exchanged in all hotels, banks and exchange offices situated almost on every corner (they are marked by the sign of the National Bank of Serbia).

Differences in rates of exchange are minimal. Currency exchange machines are situated in some places which are marked on our map of Belgrade (in the city centre, shopping centres, at the airport...). The machines exchange euro, dollar and British pound.

In most banks in Belgrade you can exchange Traveller's Cheques, American Express, Thomas Cook, VISA and Electrocheques. The post office and the majority of banks pay out Western Union money transfers.

You probably did not know that the first cash point machine (ATM) in Southern Europe was installed in Belgrade (before Italy, Spain, Greece...), in the early 1980s. Almost all goods and services everywhere can be paid by credit cards (except in green markets, news-stands and car parks). There is a great number of cash point machines all over the city where you can take your money 24 hours a day.

It is possible to use VISA, VISA Electron, MasterCard, Eurocard, Maestro, Diners Club and domestic DinaCard in Belgrade. American Express will start to be accepted in 2006.

Banks on duty

KOMERCIJALNA BANKA, Trg Nikole Pašića 2, weekdays and Saturdays from 8am to 8pm, Sundays from 9am to 3pm.

RAIFFEISENBANK, "Mercator" Shopping Centre in New Belgrade, weekdays and Saturdays from 9am to 9pm, Sundays from 9am to 5pm.

Telephone numbers for reporting the loss of card

VISA, Tel: 3011-550

MasterCard, Tel: 3010-160

Diners Club, Tel: 3440-622

Places with banks and cash point machines (ATM) on duty are marked on our map of Belgrade.

Communications

Making a phone call

The country code number for Serbia is 381, and code for Belgrade is 011.

Dialling a telephone number on the landline:

When you are calling someone in Belgrade from abroad first dial your exit country code (+), then 38111 and, in the end, the desired telephone number. When calling someone in Belgrade from another part of Serbia dial 011 and then the desired telephone number. When you are in Belgrade just dial the desired telephone number. The telephone numbers in this guide are written without the codes (except in the first chapter). If you are in Belgrade dial them without any codes, if you are calling from abroad, add the code (+38111).

When calling abroad from Belgrade on the landline, dial the exit country code for Serbia (99), then the code of the country you are calling and the desired telephone number. The telephone numbers on the landline and mobile network can be six- or seven-digit numbers.

Examples:

Calling a landline in Belgrade from abroad: +381-11-XXXXXX

Calling abroad from Belgrade: 99-outside code of your country-desired telephone number

Calling Belgrade from another part of Serbia: 011-XXXXXX

On the street you can make phone calls from "Halo" phone boxes. From them you can call abroad, on the landline or mobile network. In order to use these phone boxes you need a "Halo" phone card which is bought on news-stands or in post offices. "Halo" phone cards are sold for 200 and 300 dinars. With one "Halo" phone card of 200 dinars you can talk with England and Germany for 9 minutes, with the USA for 5 minutes, with Slovenia and Italy for 11 minutes...

There are two mobile phone operators in Serbia, Telenor (dialling code 063) and 064 Serbian Telecom (dialling code 064).

Prepay telephone numbers (PAYG) and credit for both networks can be bought on the news-stands (for 064 in the post offices, too). Credit is sold in amounts of 200, 500 and 1,000 dinars. The price of the call per minute in both networks is between 10 and 15 dinars. SMS in domestic network is 3 dinars, and around 8 dinars when sent abroad.

Calling a mobile phone number from abroad: +38163XXXXXX or +38164XXXXXX.

Calling a mobile phone number from Belgrade (from the landline or mobile telephone number) 063XXXXXX or 064XXXXXX.

When you are calling a landline from either of the two mobile networks, dial the dialling code also (011XXXXXX).

Important telephone numbers

Police - **92**
Fire department - **93**
Ambulance - **94**
Exact time - **95**
Telegrams by telephone - **96**
(7am-9pm)
Road assistance - **987**, **9800**
Phone numbers in Belgrade - **988**
Wake-up calls - **9811**
Directory enquiries service - **9812**
Emergency Room - **3618-444**
Telekom Srbija (landline and mobile network and a phone book):
www.telekom.yu
Telenor: www.telenor.co.yu

> *Note: these web presentations are in Serbian only.*

Post office

Postcode for Belgrade is 11000. Cards and letters can be dropped into postboxes (there are many types of them but they all have a **Pošta** logo) or handed in at post offices.

Post offices on duty
(daily 8am-8pm):

Pošta 01, Takovska 2
(next to Federal Parliament)
Pošta 06, Savska 2
(near the Central Railway Station)
Pošta 08, Šumadijski trg 2A
Pošta 80, Glavna 8
(in the centre of Zemun)

Courier service:

Post Express, Takovska 2;
Tel: 3607-607, 065-3607-607
(from 8am to 6pm);
www.postexpress.co.yu

DHL, Omladinskih brigada 86;
Tel: 3105-500 (from 8am to 6pm);
www.dhl.co.yu

FedEx, Autoput 22 (Motorway);
Tel: 3149-075;
www.flying-cargo.co.yu

Internet
Internet domain for Serbia is .yu

Internet cafés
- Maverik, Youth Cultural Centre, the corner of Makedonska and Dečanska Streets

- Plato, Vasina Street
on Studentski trg

- Hot Spot Cafe; Studentski trg 21

> *Internet cafés are marked on our map of Belgrade.*

Dial-up numbers for Internet connection without subscription and settings, charged over the telephone bill:
041-554-554;
username: info, password: sky
042-210-555;
username: net, password: net
The service is charged over the telephone bill.

WiFi hotspots in Belgrade
(if you have a notebook with WiFi option):

Absinthe Bar & Brasserie,
Kralja Milutina 33;

Hot Spot Café, Studentski trg 21;

Hotel Moskva, Terazije;

Federal Association of World Travellers, Bulevar Despota Stefana 7;

Restaurant "Košava", Kralja Petra 36;

Lava Bar, Kneza Miloša 77;

"Opera" Restaurant,
Obilićev venac 30;

"Veprov dah" Scottish Pub, Strahinjića Bana 52.

Newspapers, radio and TV

Foreign newspapers and magazines can be found on well-supplied news-stands on Terazije, in "Mercator" and "Super Vero" in New Belgrade, in the "IPS" bookstores (the basement of "Beogradski izlog" on Republic Square, "Mamut" at the beginning of Sremska Street). Some of the FM radio stations that mainly broadcast music are JAT Radio (95.7 MHz), Žabac Radio (101.6 MHzMHz), Idea Radio (103.3 MHZ). Currently there are about twenty national and local TV stations that can be watched in Belgrade but we think it is a waste of time to spend a short stay in Belgrade in front of the TV set. If you need to be informed, it is better to read a newspaper in one of the cafés, who knows what good will come of that.

Shopping, Souvenirs

In the tourist sense Belgrade is still waking up. That is the reason why the offer of the purpose-made souvenirs is not really large and of high-quality. Still, that does not mean you will not find some really interesting artifacts, especially if they are part of the tradition of Serbian people. We recommend taking these things from Belgrade: domestic brandy, slatko*, opanci**, šajkača***, flute****, Shepard bag, woolen socks*****, rugs or some other items of regional craftwork.

Twigs intertwined around the brandy glass carboy

You can find all this on the following spots:

"Zdravo-Živo" Shop, (to the left in the passageway) and in the underground passage on Terazije; Tel: 063-8785-988; zdravozivo@yubc.net; www.zdravozivo.co.yu

Ethnic shop of Ethnographic Museum; Studentski trg 13; Tel: 3281-888

Milma Art Centar; Karađorđeva 2-4 (Hafen Belgrad);Tel: 2634-840.

"KIRI", Peasant footwear workshop, Kaluđerica (we are not giving the address since it is too complicated for a foreign citizen to find it in the largest illegal settlement in Europe, contact them by phone); Tel: 3413-041, 063-200-825; kiri@opanci.com; www.opanci.com

Women often buy honey with nuts as a present to their men

Testija – water container

Šajkača

National footwear - opanci

T-shirts, caps and stationery with motives of Belgrade can be found in "Beoizlog" on Republic Square (Knez Mihailova 6). On a couple of stalls at the end of Knez Mihailova Street (next to the city library), handmade

Rug from Pirot

Apart from bying souvenirs, we would recommend visiting some interesting shops if you have time:

- **Adoré**, "Milenijum" Shopping Centre, entrance from Knez Mihailova Street. A wide assortment of differently-flavoured, divine, chocolate sweets "Adoré". Those who like chocolate must not miss this! 100g - 300 dinars. Tel: 2625-056

- **Flowers and Arts**, Kosančićev venac 5; Tel: 2638-257; Various interesting items for home.

- **NEVEN**, Čika Ljubina 15 (next to Australian Embassy); Tel: 2624-880; www.neven.co.yu; Unique, hand-painted, silk ties, designed by the owner of the shop, Neven Vrgoč.

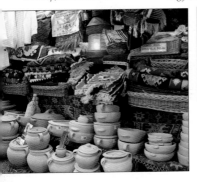

souvenirs with city motives are sold (ceramics, wood, glass). Handicrafts (knit and embroidered artifacts) are made and sold by some women in Kalemegdan Park. We recommend colourful wool sweaters.

- **Dve šmizle**, Bulevar Kralja Aleksandra 26; Tel: 3245-631; Various interesting trinkets for women.

- **Identity**, Zmaj Jovina 30; Tel: 3284-044; Original clothes, shoes, hats and purses.

Shepherd bags

If you are interested in the offer of clothes and shoes in Belgrade, look in **"Milenijum"** and **"City Passage"** Shopping Centres, as well as in the stores in Knez Mihailova Street. Prices of branded clothes are lower

than in most larger European cities. We recommend the following green markets: Kalenić (the largest assortment of products), Zeleni venac and Bajloni

Small tub for kajmak

Flute and twin flute

(because they are in the centre of the city) and the one in blok 44 in New Belgrade (the best organised one).

→ *More details on domestic brandy and slatko on pages 68 and 66.*

*Opanci are national peasant foot-wear. The sole is made of cow and the strand of sheep-hide. They are made with or without the "beak" and are as comfortable as Italian shoes.

** Šajkača is the Serbian national cap from the 18th century. It was primarily worn by šajkaši, the Serbs that fought on the side of Austria-Hungary against the Turks on the rivers Danube and Sava. Serbian soldiers wore it as a part of uniform in the First World War. Today, it is only worn by peasants in some parts of Serbia.

*** Although it is not a Serbian invention, the flute became a national instrument in time. It is made of wood (plum, elder, cornelian cherry, black locust, lilac, maple...) and produces a tender, soft sound, carrying the emotions from the soul (in other words, speaking all languages).

**** Authentic men's wear from Šumadija district: hand-embroidered shirt, stout peasant cloth embroidered vest, hand-loom weaved belt, stout peasant cloth trousers, hand-knit and embroidered socks, peasant footwear, peasant cap. Women s wear from Šumadija: hand-embroidered shirt, cotton vest hand-weaved with gold or silver thread, hand-loom weaved belt, hand-loom weaved skirt, cotton embroidered apron, hand-knit and embroidered stockings, peasant footwear.

Sightseeing

Tourist Organisation of Belgrade offers regular sightseeing tours by bus or on foot accompanied by professional guides. Information on them is available in the tourist information centre (underground passage near "Albanija" Palace; Tel: 635-622) or on www.tob.co.yu. We have chosen four interesting tours:

The Royal Compound of Karađorđević dynasty on Dedinje

Open for sightseeing from 1 April to 31 October. Duration: around 2 hours, accompanied by a tourist guide. Departure: 12, Nikole Pašića Square, Saturdays and Sundays at 10.30am and 12.30pm. By bus to Dedinje, and then a tour of the Palace park, Royal Palace and White Palace on foot.

Information and booking: The tourist information centre, underground passage near "Albanija" Palace; Tel: 635-622; e-mail: dvor@belgradetourism.co.yu; www.tob.co.yu, www.kraljevina.org

If you are coming to Belgrade by yourself (without a travel agency), it is best to book in advance your appointment for visiting the underground caves and Royal Compound, by phone or over the Internet, because you have to wait as long as 15 days for a free appointment.

Sightseeing departure points and the tourist information centre are marked on our map of Belgrade.

Sightseeing of underground caves and tunnels under Tašmajdan

About 3,000m² of underground rooms and caves up to 10m high. Admission: 100 dinars. It is organised occasionally.

Information and booking: "Izletnik" Tourist Association, Balkanska 12 (underground passage, a metal door to the left of the stairs); Tel: 063-304-817

Sightseeing from a hot-air balloon

The flight with a hot-air balloon includes organised transport to the place of departure and return after the flight, flight of 60-90 minute duration, diploma and presents, celebration on the landing spot with sparkling wine, insurance. Flying is possible every day in the year when there is no rain or snow, and the wind is not stronger than 5m/s. The balloon flies up to 1,000m high. Departure is from the plateau under Belgrade Fortress. The hot-air balloon can be rented for other purposes. Information and booking:

Balon Servis: 065-3343-434
www.balonservis.co.yu
Balon centar: 065-8119-119
www.baloncentar.com

Seightseeing from a motorised hang-glider

There is room for only one person (besides the pilot) in a motorised hang-glider. It is flown at the altitude of 50 to 600m.

"Lisičji jarak" Sports airport;
Tel: 063-8384-087; www.airzak.co.yu

Sightseeing by the "Beograd" tourist boat

Tourist Organisation of Belgrade (TOB) organises Belgrade sightseeing cruise on the Danube and the Sava, accompanied by a professional guide, from 15 May to 15 October. The river will give you the ugliest, as well as the most beautiful, view of the city. Departure is from the pier near "Jugoslavija" Hotel, the boat sails along Great War Island, Belgrade Fortress, under the bridges on the Sava to Ada Ciganlija and back. The ride takes one hour and a half.

Boat capacity: 60 places (31 places in the indoor and 29 places in the outdoor section of the boat). It is necessary to come to the pier 20-30 minutes before the departure of the boat (tickets are sold until the boat is full, so it is better to come on time). Admission: 400 dinars, children aged 6-14 and students with "Easy travel card" 200 dinars. It is possible to rent the boat for weddings and celebrations (up to 35 persons). Price: 9,000 dinars per hour.

Departures: Tuesday, Wednesday, Thursday and Friday at 6pm; Saturday and Sunday at 4pm and 6pm; Mondays - no tours.

Sports

Hunting

The hunting grounds in Serbia are among the best known in Europe. In the Belgrade surroundings there are a couple of hunting grounds for many species of big and small game.

Hunting ground of Hunting Club Zemun - 30,200ha area, game: roe-deer, boar, rabbit, pheasant and partridge.

"Crni lug" hunting ground; 973ha area, deer game and boar are bred and hunted.

"Dobanovački zabran" hunting ground; 1125ha area, game: mouflon, fallow deer, roe-deer, boar and pheasant.

Hunting area of Pančevačk rit and Slanci-Veliko Selo; 39,390ha area, game: wild geese.

Hunting ground on the territory of Grocka municipality; 28,674ha area, game: boar, roe-deer and pheasant.

Information:

Hunting Federation of Serbia, Alekse Nenadovića 19/II; Tel: 3443-284

JP "Srbijašume", Tel: 3611-083

"Srbijašume turs", Tel: 2454-467

Hunting Club Zemun, Braće Ribar 69; Tel: 8480-419

Hunting season:

European red deer (Cervus elaphus L.) 1 August - 14 February
European roe deer (Capreolus capreolus L.) 1 May - 30 September
Chamois (Rupicapra rupicapra L.) 1 August - 31 January
White fronted goose (Anser albifrons Sc.) 1 October - 31 January
Wild duck (Anas spp.) 1 September - 31 January
Partridge (Perdix perdix L.) 15 October - 30 November
Quail (Coturnix coturnix L.) 1 August - 30 September
Pheasant (Phasianus spp.) 16 October - 14 January
Bald coot (Fulica altra L.) 1 September - 31 January
Woodcock (Scolopax rusticola L.) 1 October - 31 January
Woodpigeon (Columba palumbus L.) 1 August - 31 January
Turtle-dove (Streptopelia turtur L.) 1 August - 30 September
Collared dove (S. decaocto E. Friv.) 1 August - 30 September

Hunting bears, wild cats and wolves is banned throughout the year (except in special cases when traditional wolf hunts are organised).

Regulations for foreign hunters:

Hunting weapons and ammunition (to a certain quantity) can be temporarily brought into Serbia only in case of an organised hunt (organised by the Hunting Federation or other authorised organisations). Foreign citizens coming to hunt in Serbia on the border pay a tax for all kinds of hunting weapons, 6 EUR a piece. For a ten day hunting trip each hunter is allowed to import up to 1000 hunting rifle cartridges. Foreign citizens can rent hunting weapons on the hunting ground where they are staying at the rate of 5 EUR for a shotgun and 10 EUR for a carbine per day.

Hunting weapons are rented on the condition that hunters possess a valid permit for the same caliber of arms in the country they are coming from. For hunting dogs entering Serbia and Montenegro the same rules apply as for pets. When importing animals it is necessary to submit a health-check certificate (done in the country the person is coming from) and to acquire, on the border, a certificate of a carried out veterinary-sanitary control. A hunting dog can be rented at the rate of 10 EUR per day.

Hunters-tourists can take the hunted game and game trophies out of the country only if a certificate was issued (for game), i.e. trophy certificate (for trophies). When exporting hunting trophies and venison out of Serbia and Montenegro it is necessary to possess a veterinary certificate, issued by the Republic Veterinary Inspectorate. The Hunting Federation or the organisation you are staying with will help you with this procedure.Useful address: www.yuclaytarget.org.yu

Fishing

In the vicinity of Belgrade fishing

is possible on the rivers Sava and Danube, the lake on Ada Ciganlija, as well as in the waters of Pančevački rit. Individual fishing is possible but a license valid for one to seven days must be procured beforehand.
Information: Belgrade Sports-fishing Association, Milovana Milovanovića 4; Tel: 3613-590

Fishing season:

Sterlet (Acipenser L.)
1 June - 31 March
Brown trout (Salmo trutta m. fario L.) 2 March - 30 September
Lake trout (Salmo trutta m. lacustris L.) 2 March - 30 September
Pike-perch (Lucioperca volgesis)
1 May - 28 February
European catfish (Silurus glanis L.)
16 June - 30 May
Carp (Cyprinus carip. L.)
1 June - 30 March
Northern Pike (Esox lucius L.)
1 April - 30 September

Shooting range

Sports centre Kovilovo, the best shooting range in Europe. The complex comprises six shooting ranges for Skeet, Trap and Double Trap disciplines, as well as one compact shooting ground. You can bring your own equipment or rent it (20 EUR/day is a rifle, 5 EUR/day series of 25 pigeons). Sports and hunting equipment shop, school of shooting, boxes for dogs.

12 km north of the city.
Tel: 3328-908, Fax: 3328-726;
bgsck@bgsck.org.yu;
www.bgsck.org.yu

Squash

SquashLand, Pionirski grad in Košutnjak; Tel: 3548-040, 065-8555-558; Open: 10am-11pm; Two courts, sauna, massage, café, equipment renting and selling, squash school;
www.squashland.com

ATV

Extreme park Gravel. Two ground tracks: the first, 750m long (not so sharp

but fast bends), the second 1250m long (moto-cross track with 18 bends and 5 jumps). Six ATV vehicles Kawasaki KFX 700 and 400. There are tracks for BMX and mountain bike, a café and a car park inside the complex. It is situated alongside the motorway in the direction to the airport, on the right (1km from the pedestrian walkway with the inscription "Ikarbus" there is an unmarked turning to the country road and after 200m you arrive to the park).
www.atvgravel.com

Carting

1. Autokomerc Carting Centre, outdoor track alongside the motorway in the direction from the airport to the city (on the right). The track with FIA C licence 803m long, 8m wide with 18 bends. The season is from March to October, every day except

Mondays. The track is lighted for night driving, too. A ten-minute drive (with stopwatch) is 10 euros, an hour is 50 euros; the track can be rented. There is a carting school.

2.Flojd, indoor electrocarting track under the Mostar loop. A seven-minute drive is 4 euros to 6pm, after 6pm and at weekends - 5 euros. Whole track renting for 20 persons, for one hour, is around 85 euros. A glass wall 25m wide separates the track from the diner, so your friends can watch you while you are driving. The speed is limited until they see how good you are at driving. Open: 10am-1am. Car park. Tel: 065-2535-693;
www.floyd-kart.co.yu

Fitness centres

The recommended fitness centres have got a great variety of different fitness programs, excellent-quality equipment, weights and cardio systems.

1. Extreme Gym, Cvijićeva 1 (hidden a little from the street, inside the business centre);
Tel: 2768-255 (8-24h);
www.x3mgym.com

2. Power Gym, Steve Todorovića 32 (on Banovo brdo); Tel: 3545-935 (9-22h); www.powergym.co.yu

Paintball

Simulation of firefights. Two courts: the outdoor one is on Ada Ciganlija, and the indoor one in the unfinished seven-floor building near Studentski dom in New Belgrade. You can form your own team or join another.

Paintball klub Arena No 1;
Tel: 063-7796-796;
e-mail: info@arenaNo1.co.yu;
www.arenaNo1.co.yu

Sports climbing

"Vertical" Club. Artificial wall is placed on Ada Ciganlija. There is no age limit, and no previous knowledge is needed, because the

necessary instructions are given on the spot. The climbers are, naturally, secured with ropes.

Club membership (through which you get the right to use the wall daily) is around 20 euros.
www.vertical.org.yu

Cable for waterskiing

It is situated on the Makiš side of Ada Ciganlija. Tel: 3058-066, 063-8599-986;
Open: 9am-11pm

Water Park

During 2006 two large water parks should be opened, one along the Sava bank in blok 44 in New Belgrade, and the other in the sports centre Kovilovo (see "Shooting range").

Horse Racing

On Sundays on Belgrade Racecourse, the oldest sports establishment in town (opened before the First World War, and has not changed a lot since then, only the main stands have burnt down in the fire). The season lasts from April to October. There is a horse-riding school, too.
www.hipodrombeograd.co.yu

Golf

"Beograd" Golf Club. A nine-hole golf-course on Ada Ciganlija, there is a golf school, too.
Tel: 3551-559, 3056-837;
www.golfclub.co.yu

Jet-Ski

"Savski biser" Nautical Club. The Sava quay, at the end of blok 45 in New Belgrade; Tel: 3186-503.

Football

If you are a genuine football fan be sure to come to a football derby between Red Star (Crvena Zvezda) (European and World Champion in 1991) and Partizan, at least once in you life. Fantastic atmosphere and rivalry on the stands, as well as on the pitch. Half of the city (or a bit more) supports Red Star, and a half of the city supports Partizan. The colours of Red Star are red and white (the supporters are always on the north stands), and black and white of Partizan (the supporters are always on the south stands). First time on the derby it is best to be on the west or the east stand. Their stadiums are next to each other (marked on our map of Belgrade). The stadium of Red Star is the largest in the city and it has 54,000 seats.

Basketball

The best basketball in the world, after NBA, is played in Belgrade (this was confirmed a couple of times in European and World competitions). There is a basketball court in every neighbourhood in the city where you can try out your skills with the local boys and learn something along the way. Belgrade has the largest basketball hall in Europe - "Belgrade arena" (alongside the motorway in New Belgrade, 20,000 seats). The two best basketball teams in the city are Red Star and Partizan, of course. There is the same rivalry between them as in football. Their games are played in "Pionir" Sports Centre, Čarli Čaplina 39.

Skating

"Pionir" Sports Centre – Ice hall. Recreational skating, skating school and hockey on ice. Recreation timetable is usually on working days in the evenings, and at weekends during the day, too. Čarli Čaplina 39; Tel: 766-667. You can check the timetable on the site: www.tasmajdan.co.yu

Swimming Pools

The swimming season on the outdoor pools is from June to the end of August, and the indoor ones are open all year round. Apart from recreation timetable, there are timetables for aquabic, as well as the swimming school for children and non-swimmers. Some establishments, apart from changing rooms and showers, have a sauna, massage parlour,

"Tašmajdan", Beogradska 71;
Tel: 3240-901; www.tasmajdan.co.yu

"Banjica", Crnotravska 4;
Tel: 668-700

"Milan Gale Muškatirović",
Tadeuša Košćuška 63 (Dorćol);
Tel: 2622-866

"11. april", near Students' Residence in New Belgrade; Tel: 2672-939

"Košutnjak", Kneza Višeslava 72;
Tel: 3555-461

> Note: Swimming in the Danube is not recommended beacuse of the strong main current and numerous whirlpools.
> Belgraders (who do not mind the mud and the strange colour of the water) swim in the river Sava, in the area of Ada Ciganlija and Ada Međica. They do not suffer any consequences, but we are not sure that we could guarantee the same to you.

fitness centre, solarium... We cannot boast with successes in swimming but we are proficient in waterpolo. If you want to swim in one of the pools where European and World champions practise, visit the sports-recreational centres:

Tennis and basketball courts inside Belgrade Fortress

Day Trips

The Šargan Eight

One of the most beautiful railway lines of narrow gauge in the world runs through Mokra Gora and on the slopes of Tara, Zlatibor and Šargan. It is called the "eight" because a steep ascent is successfully surmounted on a short distance. Fare for adults is 500 dinars. It is possible to hire the

train (with Diesel-locomotive 50,000 dinars, with steam locomotive 120,000 dinars). Since you are in this area visit Drvengrad on Mećavnik, a village built by the famous director Emir Kusturica.

Additional information: Tel. 3616-928, 3618-353 (8am-4pm); sarganska. osmica@yurail.co.yu; www.yurail.co.yu

Museum Train "Romantika"

Steam engine and authentic carriages of I, II and III class from the beginning of the last century. Serbian Railway takes you to romantic, one-day excursions on weekends, from May to October. Destinations are: Sremski Karlovci, Bela Crkva, Vrnjačka Banja, Palić…

Fare includes seat reservation, sightseeing in the city, transport of one bicycle. In winter (at weekends) the train goes on a circular tour around Belgrade for two hours, together with the visit to the Blue train.

Additional information:
Tel. 3616-928, 3618-353 (8am-4pm);
romantika@yurail.co.yu;
www.yurail.co.yu

foto Zoran Verešić

The Blue Train

The Blue train is a popular name for a special train used for the needs of Josip Broz Tito, the late president of FR Yugoslavia. Over 60 world statesmen travelled by the Blue Train. It was specially redecorated for the journey of Queen Elizabeth II through Yugoslavia in October 1972. Formal parlour with a dining-room (where it is possible to show films), three salon cars with suits and a restaurant seat 92 people in all. The train interior is made, mostly, of wood. Mahogany, pear and walnut tree were used, and the salons and corridors are decorated with inlaid wood. The interior is completed with quality materials: woolen rugs, plush, silk, in authentic Art Deco style. Journeys are arranged on the basis of special contracts, according to the desired destination. Prices of one-day renting of the Blue Train (salon, formal parlour, restaurant car and engine car) on some of the possible destinations: Belgrade-Užice-Belgrade from 2347 EUR; Belgrade-Subotica-Belgrade from 2260 EUR; Belgrade-Vrnjačka Banja-Belgrade from 2741 EUR

Information: Tel. 3616-928, 3618-353 (8am-4pm); plavi.voz@yurail.co.yu; www.yurail.co.yu
Tourist Organisation of Belgrade - TOB: www.belgradetourism.org.yu www.tob.co.yu
Tourist Organisation of Serbia - TOS: www.serbia-tourism.org

Cultural and Artistic Events

Flower Fair on Nikole Pašića Square (held once in spring and once in autumn)

1 January: **The Street of the Open Heart**. New Year's Carnival in Svetogorska Street. The programme for children (actors, musicians, Santa Clause) and adults (cooked brandy and brine for a good morning) starts at noon.

13 January: **Celebration of (Serbian)**

New Year by the Julian calendar. Special programme in the inns.

19 January: **Twelfth-day**. Traditional diving for the "Epiphany Cross" on Ada Ciganlija (in the lake) and on the Danube (Zemun quay). The bravest of young men test their stamina and speed in icy waters.

End of February-beginning of March: **FEST**. International, non-competitive film festival. It takes place in "Sava" Centre, with additional programs in Youth Cultural Centre and the Museum of Yugoslav Film Archives.

March: **Belgrade Festival of Documentary and Short Film**. International, competitive. Categories: documentary, short feature film, animated film, experimental film. Film and video techniques.
www.kratkimetar.org.yu

March: **International Competition of Young Musicians**. Young artists (up to 30 years old) compete in the following categories: voice, composition, instrumental soloists, chamber orchestras.
www.music-competition.co.yu

April: **Belgrade Marathon**. Apart from the international marathon there is a half-marathon and a joy-race for amateurs. People run through the streets of Belgrade, on a Saturday morning. www.bgmarathon.com

May: **Festival of Stuntmen**. International meeting of stuntmen with the demonstrations of stunts. It takes place in the park between Brankov Bridge and "Ušće" Business Centre. www.kaskaderi.org.yu

Thursday, 40 days after Easter (Ascension Day - Spasovdan): **Belgrade slava* - Ascension Day**

Liturgy. The religious procession starts from Vaznesenjska crkva (Church of the Ascension), goes along Kralja Milana Street to Terazije, the first stop for the prayer for the health of Belgrade citizens. Then it continues along Knez Mihailova and Kralja Petra Streets to The Orthodox Cathedral. The second stop is there for the prayers for alleviation of suffering, health and prosperity. The circle is closed in the yard of the Church of the Ascension with the prayer for the dead heroes of Belgrade. A great number of Belgrade citizens participate in this religious procession.

June: **International Chivalry Tour-**

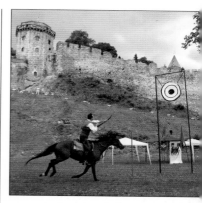

nament. Parade of the participants, demonstration of martial arts, horse fighting, archery contest, fight on the log, medieval music and dance... Display of medieval artistic craftsmanship (calligraphy, painting, heraldry, iconography, armourer's trade). It takes place in Lower town below Belgrade Fortress.
www.svibor.co.yu

June-July: **Kalemegdan Dusks**. Concerts of popular classical music in Kalemegdan, on the plateau of the Institute for Cultural Heritage Conservation and in the music pavillion. Most frequently in the late afternoon hours.

July-August: **BELEF** - Belgrade Summer Festival. Theatre, dance, visual arts, concerts, performances, installations of native and foreign artists on Belgrade streets, squares and various unusual places. www.belef.org

August: **Beerfest**. Festival of beer and music on the plateau of Lower

town below Belgrade Fortress. About thirty varieties of beer on the stalls of the manufacturers. During the day there is a family atmosphere, and in the evening the rock concerts start and last far into the night. Cheerful atmosphere and positive energy. The stalls are open from 10am-4am. www.belgradebeerfest.com

August: **Boat Carnival**. A whole-day party on the river: rowers, boats,

sailing-boats, jet-skis, skiers. On land: Gypsy and tamburitza orchestras, fish soup and pork roast. Fireworks after nightfall.

September: **BITEF**. International festival of the new theatrical tendencies. Competitive. It takes place in theatres with several additional programs. www.bitef.co.yu

September: **Belgrade Tango Festival**. During the day master classes of famous dancing couples from Argentina and other countries. In

the night, concerts and milongas in interesting places. www.belgradetangofestival.com

October: **BEMUS**. International music event in the area of classical, ethnic and contemporary music. Guests are world famous soloists and conductors. It takes place in "Sava" Centre, Ilija M. Kolarac Foundation and other venues. www.bemus.co.yu

September: **Festival of Nitrite Film**. Museum of Yugoslav Film Archives

is the only institution in the world that shows the selection from the archives of "inflammable" films every year.

October: The **Joy of Europe**. International meeting of children where they show the artistic craftsmanship from their countries. It takes place in Children's Cultural Centre, "Sava" Centre and other outdoor places in the city. www.joyofeurope.org.yu

October: **Jazz Festival**. Famous world and native jazz players in close contact with the audience in Youth Cultural Centre.

October: **October Salon**. Presents domestic authors in the areas of visual and applied arts and design, together with the guests from abroad. It takes place in a couple of city museums and galleries. It lasts the whole month. www.oktobarskisalon.org

October: **Belgrade Book Fair**. International fair of publishers where you can buy books. Every year a different country is an honourary guest of the fair. www.sajam.co.yu

December: **Festival of Underwater Film**. An international, competitive festival, one of the largest in the world. It includes film production, underwater photography, students' and art works. It is held in the large theatre in Youth Cultural Centre and the cinema of the Museum of Yugoslav Film Archives.

31 December: **New Year`s Celebration**. Organised celebration on the

main city squares and streets, with live music and fireworks. All restaurants and discos prepare special programmes. Due to a great number of foreign visitors, it is best to book a hotel room at least one month before the holidays.

*Belgrade Slava

"When I came, I found the most beautiful place of old, The too large a city of Belgrade, Which was devastated and forlorn by the circumstances. I raised it and dedicated it to the Most Holy Virgin."

Despot Stefan Lazarević

Since Despot Stefan Lazarević dedicated Belgrade to the Most Holy Virgin and gave it the status of a capital in 1403, the city took Ascension Day - Spasovdan for its slava. This votive slava symbolically suggests the resurrection - ascension of the city from the ashes and the faith in hope and future. On the celebration of Ascension Day in 1939 the city of Belgrade was honoured with the highest war decoration – Order of Karađorđe's Star with Swords of IV degree.

→ *You can find out what slava is and how it is celebrated on page 130.*

31 December: New Year's Celebration. Organised celebration on the main city squares and streets, with live music and fireworks. All restaurants and discos prepare special programmes. Due to a great number of foreign visitors, it is best to book a hotel room at least one month before the holidays.

Local Customs

- Belgraders are very warm and friendly. They do not have prejudices against foreign citizens (no matter where they come from) or other races. You can make acquaintances or friends (yes, true friends) even on the first day of your stay. Everyone will be glad to help you with the directions in the city, and it is not unusual for someone to invite you for a coffee or lunch at their home.

- Belgraders shake hands and say "Zdravo" (Hello) or "Ćao" (Hi) when they meet, and if they have not seen each other for a long time

they kiss three times on the cheeks.

- Being late is a usual thing. If you are fifteen minutes late, it means that you are on time. Almost no film or theatre premiere, exhibition opening or concert starts on time. The visitors use the opportunity to say hello to their friends and gossip

about their enemies, so they ignore the bell calling for entrance for a long time. Rock concerts are usually more than one hour late.

- When toasting, Belgraders look each other in the eye, clink glasses and say "Živeli" ("Cheers"). At meals you say "Prijatno" ("Enjoy your meal").

- The bill in the inn is not shared. The one who invites you to have a drink or lunch pays the bill. If there was a chance meeting that ended in the inn, friends are known to start a fight about who will pick the tab (everybody insists on treating the others).

- Swearing is a usual means of

communication and there is a great variety of swear words (they often consist of a couple of complex sentences). Even friends swear each other. Only in intonation and the look will you see whether someone is swearing because they are threatening you or they are glad to see you.

- Prostitution and marihuana are illegal. Avoid the trouble that could spoil your vacation. Since you are a foreigner in the city you will find it

hard to recognise policemen in civilian clothes.

- Tatoos, pearsing, girls with shaved heads can be seen in the streets, but men who hold hands and kiss on the mouth cannot. Homosexuals are tolerated and accepted as long as they do not show their feelings in public. If you have that kind of affinities save them for the hotel room because the passers-by can be hostile towards you.

- It is not well-mannered to phone someone before 10am (unless you are sure that the person is at work) and after 10pm. If someone mentions a meeting at lunchtime, it probably means between 3pm and 5pm. Dinner is usually scheduled between 8pm and 10pm.

- When you are visiting somebody at their home it is a custom to take a packet of coffee and a bottle of drink to the hosts, and a chocolate for every child.

- Every family celebrates a saint.

When they became Christian the Serbs chose their family patrons among the Saints. Celebration of the day dedicated to a saint is called "slava" (the meaning in Serbian is "the praise"). For that day people prepare "slavski kolač" (a specially decorated bread) and "žito", serve red wine and light a candle. The closest relatives and friends come as guests. It is a great honour to be invited to somebody's "slava".

- You will notice that during hot summer and cold winter days (i.e. throughout the year) many premises are stuffy and not aired. This is because the Serbs are very sensitive to **promaja** (the movement of the air between two openings on the opposite ends of the room) and they often get sick from it (believe it or not).

Medical Care

If you have some minor health problems, we advise you to go to one of the private practices. They are more expensive but you will avoid waiting in line in the crowded state hospitals and dealing with bureaucrats dressed as doctors. It is best to take out international medical insurance before the journey and you will not have to worry about the medical treatment expenses. For trauma and emergency interventions Ambulance Service and Emergency Room are at your disposal. For emergency dental treatment we pointed out two places on duty 24 hours a day, but if you can bear it and make an appointment during proper working hours, from Monday to Friday, we recommend the surgery "Jovanović" on Dorćol.

Useful addresses and telephone numbers:

EMERGENCY CENTRE (0-24h), Pasterova 2; Tel: 3618-444

AMBULANCE (0-24h), Bulevar Franše D'Eperea 5; tel. 94

AMBULANCE (7pm-7am): Children's clinic, Bulevar Franše D'Eperea 5; Tel: 3615-001 ext. 114

Night clinic "Stari grad", Kralja Petra 10A; Tel: 3282-351

Night clinic "Novi Beograd" Blok 44; Tel: 1769-794

Medical institutions on duty:

CLINICAL CENTRE OF SERBIA, Pasterova 2; Tel: 3617-777

MEDICAL CENTRE "ZVEZDARA", Dimitrija Tucovića 161; Tel: 3406-333, 3406-969

MEDICAL CENTRE "Dr DRAGIŠA MIŠOVIĆ", Heroja Milana Tepića 1; Tel: 2667-122, 2660-222

MEDICAL CENTRE "ZEMUN", Zemun, Vukova 9; Tel: 2612-616, 2106-106

MEDICAL CENTRE "BEŽANIJSKA KOSA", Bežanijska kosa bb; Tel: 2601-322, 2601-320

MILITARY MEDICAL ACADEMY, Crnotravska 17; Tel: 2661-122, 2662-755, 2663-660

Pharmacies on duty 24 hours a day:

PRVI MAJ, Kralja Milana 9; Tel: 3240-533

SVETI SAVA, Nemanjina 2; Tel: 2643-170

ZEMUN, Glavna 34; Tel: 2618-582

FARMANEA, Republic Square; Tel: 3344-923

GALENIKA, Senjski trg 7 Zemun; Tel: 108-848

PHARMANOVA, Nevesinjska 17, Tel. 4447-993

HERBAL PHARMACY, Tadeuša Košćučkog 1; Tel: 2182-112

Dentists on duty 24 hours a day:

STARI GRAD, Obilićev venac 30; Tel: 635-236

NOVI BEOGRAD, Goce Delčeva 30, Tel: 2222-100; Nehruova 53 (block 44), Tel: 2095-200; Omladinskih brigada 4 ("Medicina rada"), Tel: 2095-400

Some private practices (medical specialists, diagnostic instruments):

Anlave, Bežanijska kosa; Tel: 2271-944, 3175-929; www.anlave.co.yu

Bel Medic, Viktora Igoa 1, Tel: 3065-888; Koste Jovanovića 87, Tel: 3091-000 (0-24h)

Dr Ristić, Narodnih Heroja 38 Novi Beograd; Tel: 2693-287, 063-205-764 (0-24h)

Euromedic, Cara Dušana 37; Tel: 3346-896

Vizim, Knez Miletina 36; Tel: 3391-721

Dentist's surgery "Jovanović", Dunavski kej 11; Tel: 2636-065

Emergency Room, hospitals on duty, dentist's surgeries and pharmacies are marked on our map of Belgrade.

Useful Addresses

Embassies

Albania, Bulevar Kneza Aleksandra Karađorđevića 25a; Tel: 3066-642; alembassy_Belgrade@hotmail.com
Algeria, Maglajska 26b; Tel: 3671-211; ambalg@eunet.yu
Angola, Vase Pelagića 32; Tel: 3693-270; embang@yubc.net
Argentina, Knez Mihailova 24/I; Tel: 2622-541; embaryu@eunet.yu
Australia, Čika Ljubina 13; Tel: 3303-400; belgrade.embassy@dfat.gov.au
Austria, Kneza Sime Markovića 2; Tel: 3031-956; Belgrad-OB@bmaa.gv.at
Belarus, Deligradska 13; Tel: 3616-938; sam@belembassy.org
Belgium, Krunska 18; Tel: 3230-018; embassy@belgium.org.yu
Bosnia and Herzegovina, Milana Tankosića 8; Tel: 3291-995; ambasadabih@yubc.net
Brazil, Krunska 14; Tel: 3239-781;

brasbelg@eunet.yu
Bulgaria, Birčaninova 26; Tel: 3613-980; bulgamb@eunet.yu
Canada, Kneza Miloša 75; Tel: 3063-000; bgrad@dfait-maeci.gc.ca
Check Republic, Bulevar Kralja Aleksandra 22; Tel: 3230-133; belgrade@embassy.mzv.cz
Congo, Diplomatska kolonija 3; Tel: 2664-131; ambardcbelgrade@yahoo.fr
Croatia, Kneza Miloša 62; Tel: 3610-535; croambg@eunet.yu (Konzulat, Sime Lozanića 11; Tel: 3670-078)
Cuba, Ljube Jovanovića 9b; Tel: 3692-441; emcubayu@eunet.yu
Cyprus, Diplomatska kolonija 9; Tel: 3672-725; cyembassy@sezampro.yu
Denmark, Neznanog junaka 9a;

Tel: 3670-443; begamb@um.dk
Egypt, Andre Nikolića 12; Tel: 2650-585; egemb@sbb.co.yu
Finland, Birčaninova 29; Tel: 3065-400; finembas@eunet.yu
France, Pariska 11; Tel: 3023-500; ambafr_1@eunet.yu
Germany, Kneza Miloša 74-76;

Tel: 3064-300; germemba@eunet.yu (Konzulat, Birčaninova 19a; Tel: 3064-400; germcons@tehnicom.net)
Ghana, Ognjena Price 50; Tel: 3440-856; ghana@eunet.yu
Greece, Francuska 33; Tel: 3226-523; office@greekemb.co.yu (Konzulat, Strahinjića Bana 76; Tel: 3341-507)
Great Britain, Resavska 46; Tel: 2645-055; ukembbg@eunet.yu
Guinea, Ohridska 4; Tel: 3444-840; ambaguineebelgrade@eunet.yu
Holland, Simina 29; Tel: 2023-900; belgrade@minbuza.nl
Hungary, Krunska 72; Tel: 2440-472; hunemblg@eunet.yu (Konzulat, Vladete Kovačevića 3; Tel: 3691-974)
India, Ljutice Bogdana 8; Tel: 2664-127; indemb@eunet.yu
Indonesia, Bulevar Kneza Aleksandra Karađorđevića 18; Tel: 3674-062; kombeojo@eunet.yu
Iran, Ljutice Bogdana 40; Tel: 3674-360; iran-emb@bitsyu.net
Iraq, Pukovnika Purića 4; Tel: 467-508; ambas_ik@eunet.yu
Italia, Birčaninova 11; Tel: 3066-100; office@italy.org.yu
Izrael, Bulevar Kneza Aleksandra Karađorđevića 47; Tel: 3672-400; press@BELGRADE.mfa.gov.il
Japan, Genex apartmani - Vladimira Popovića 6; Tel: 3012-800; protocol@jpemb.org.yu
Lebanon, Diplomatska kolonija 5;

Tel: 3675-153; ambaleb@eunet.yu
Lybia, Sime Lozanića 6;
Tel: 2663-445; libyaamb@eunet.yu
Macedonia, Gospodar Jevremova 34;
Tel: 3284-924; macemb@eunet.yu
Malaysia, Genex apartments Vladimira Popovića 6; Tel: 3113-570;
mwbelgrade@scnet.yu
Mexico, Ljutice Bogdana 5;
Tel: 3674-170; embamex@net.yu
Morocco, Sanje Živanović 4;
Tel: 3690-288; sifamabe@eunet.yu
Myanmar, Kneza Miloša 72;
Tel: 3619-114; mebel@sezampro.yu
Norway, Užička 43; Tel: 3670-404;
emb.belgrade@mfa.no
Pakistan, Bulevar Kneza Aleksandra Karađorđevića 62; Tel: 2661-676;
parepbeograd@yubc.net
Palestine, Maglajska 14;
Tel: 3671-407; ambpal@eunet.yu
Peru, Terazije 1/II; Tel: 3221-197;
leprubelgrado@b92. net
Poland, Kneza Miloša 38;
Tel: 2065-301; ambrpfrj@eunet.yu
Portugal, Vladimira Gaćanovića 4;
Tel: 2662-895; portugalambs@sbb.co.yu
The Republic of South Korea,
Užička 32; Tel: 3674-225;
mail@koreanemb.org.yu
Romania, Kneza Miloša 70;
Tel: 3618-327; ambelgro@infosky.net
Russia, Deligradska 32, Katićeva 8-10;
Tel: 3611-323, 2641-656;
ambarusk@eunet.yu
Slovakia, Bulevar umetnosti 18;
Tel: 3010-000; embassy@belehrad.mfa.sk
Slovenia, Zmaj Jovina 33a;
Tel: 3284-458; vbg@mzz-dkp.gov.si
Spain, Prote Mateje 45;
Tel: 3440-231; embajada@sezampro.yu
Sweden, Ledi Pedžet 2; Tel: 2069-200;
ambassaden.belgrad@foreign.ministry.se
Switzerland, Birčaninova 27;
Tel: 3065-820;
vertretung@bel.rep.admin.ch

Syria, Aleksandra Stamboliskog 13;
Tel: 2666-124; syremb@net.yu
Tunisia, Vase Pelagića 19;
Tel: 3691-961; at.belgr@eunet.yu
Turkey, Krunska 1; Tel: 3332-400;
turem@eunet.yu
The Ukraine, Bulevar oslobođenja 87;
Tel: 3978-987; emb_sm@mfa.gov.ua
USA, Kneza Miloša 50; Tel: 3619-344;
Consularbelgrd@state.gov
Vatikan, Svetog Save 24;
Tel: 3085-356; nunbel@eunet.yu
Zimbabve, Tolstojeva 51;
Tel: 3672-996; zimbegd@eunet.yu

Consulates

China, Perside Milenković 9,
Tel: 3693-163; Ljube Jovanovića 5,
Tel: 2651-630;
Chinaemb_yu@mail.mfa.gov.cn

Ecuador, Graničarska 8/III;
Tel: 3440-135; cecuador@ptt.yu

Gabon, Takovska 20; Tel: 3233-882

Seychelles, Beogradskog bataljona 42;
Tel: 3547-309

Roman Catholic Church

Church of Christ the King,
Krunska 23; Tel: 3232-308
Belgrade Archbishopic -
Archiepiscopal Ordinate, Svetozara
Markovića 20; Tel: 3032-246;
e-mail: nadbisbg@eunet.yu

Islamic religious community and Bajrakli Mosque

Gospodar Jevremova 11; Tel: 2622-428;
Mufti of Islamic community,
Tel: 2622-337; www.izs.org.yu
Bajrakli Mosque was built in the
Ottoman times in 1575. It was named
Bajrakli after the flag (barjak means
flag) that was put out as a sign for si-
multaneous beginning of prayer in all
mosques. Today it is the only active
mosque in Belgrade.

Jewish community and the Synagogue

The written sources on Jews have
been present in Belgrade since the
16th century. Ashkenazi Jews who
came from the countries of Western
Europe and who carried German cul-
ture, settled along the bank of the
Sava. Sephardic Jews, exiled from
Spain in 1492, settled in the area of
Dorćol. There is a choir "Braća Baruh"
in Belgrade which started performing
in 1879 as the Serbian-Jewish Choir.
Belgrade Jewish Municipality and
Jewish Historical Museum,
Kralja Petra 71a; Tel: 2622-449
Synagogue, Maršala Birjuzova 19
Jewish cemetery, Mije Kovačevića 1;
Tel: 768-250

Translators

**Association of Technical and
Scientific Translators of Serbia**,
Kičevska 9; Tel: 4442-997
Institute for Foreign Languages,
Gospodar Jovanova 35;
Tel: 2623-022, 2623-034

Tourism

Tourist information centres:

- "Nikola Tesla" Airport (9am-8pm),
Tel: 2097-638

- Central Railway Station (9am-8pm,
Saturdays 9am-5pm, Sundays closed),
Tel: 3612-732

- Terazije, underground passage at
"Albanija" Palace (9am-8pm, Satur-
days 9am-5pm, Sundays 10am-4pm),
Tel: 635-622

- Makedonska 5, (9-21h, Saturdays 9-
17h, Sundays 10-16h), Tel: 3343-460

- The Sava pier near Brankov bridge
(March - November)

Tourist Organisation of Belgrade - TOB:
www.tob.co.yu

Tourist Organisation of Zemun, Zmaj
Jovina 14, Tel: 192-094

Tourist Guide Association, Dečanska
8/V, Tel: 3235-910; vodicisr@yubc.net

Tourist Organisation of Serbia - TOS:
www.serbia-tourism.org

YUTA - Business Association of Travel
Agencies: www.yuta.co.yu

Ministry of trade, tourism and services,
Nemanjina 22-26; Tel: 3618-852;
www.3inttu.sr.gov.yu

Belgrade Fortress,
www.beogradskatvrdjava.co.yu

Receptive travel agencies:

- PUTNIK, Dragoslava Jovanovića 1;
Tel: 3232-591, Faks: 3244-505; inco-
ming@putnik.com; www.putnik.com

- KON TIKI TRAVEL, Beogradska
71; Tel: 3231-077, Faks: 3244-927; in-
fo@kontiki.co.yu; www.kontiki.co.yu

- GLOB METROPOLITEN TOURS,
Dositejeva 26; Tel: 2181-181;
glob@metropoliten.com;
www.metropoliten.com

- JAT AIR LIFT, Bulevar umetnosti
16; Tel: 2138-899, Faks: 2145-640;
airlift@jat.com; www.jat-airlift.co.yu

- TOURIST CENTRE KOPAONIK,
Vladimira Popovića 8; Tel: 3111-166,
Faks: 3111-803; kopaonik@icg.co.yu;
www.genex.co.yu

Lost property office

Studentski trg 18; Tel: 2182-302;
open working days 8am-3.30pm.

Ticket vendors for theatre plays, concerts and various other events

Bilet servis, Trg Republike 5;
Tel: 3033-311, www.biletservis.co.yu
Ticket Line, Strahinjića Bana 27,
Tel: 2030-570, www.ticketline.co.yu

Concert Halls

Belgrade Philharmonic Orchestra, Studentski trg 11; Tel: 3282-977; www.bgf.co.yu
Dom sindikata, Trg Nikole Pašića 5;
Tel: 3234-224
Sava Centre, Milentija Popovića 9
(New Belgrade); www.savacentar.com
Ilije M. Kolarca Foundation,
Studentski trg 5; Tel: 630-550;
www.kolarac.co.yu

Foreign Cultural Centres

American Corner,
Svetozara Markovića 23-25; Tel: 3231-404
British Council,
Terazije 8; Tel: 3023-800;
www.britishcouncil.org/yugoslavia
Canadian Cultural Centre,
Kneza Miloša 75; Tel: 3063-000
French Cultural Centre, Zmaj Jovina
11; Tel: 3023-600; www.ccf.org.yu
"Goethe" Institute (German Cultural Centre), Knez Mihailova 50;
Tel: 633-247; www.goethe.de/belgrad
"Cervantes" Institute (Spanish Cultural Centre), Čika Ljubina 19;
Tel: 632-573; www.belgrado.cervantes.es
Italian Institute, Njegoševa 47/III;
Tel: 2447-217; www.italcultbg.org.yu
Russian Centre for Culture and Science, Kraljice Natalije 33;
Tel: 2642-178; www.rcnk.co.yu

Theatres *(Pozorište)*

The most frequent genres of the plays on the repertoire are shown together with the address. Some theatres have a couple of stages.

Atelje 212 (drama, comedy),
Svetogorska 21; Tel: 3247-342;
www.atelje212.co.yu

Beogradsko dramsko pozorište (drama), Mileševska 64a; Tel: 2837-000;
www.bdp.co.yu
Bitef Teatar (modern dance), Skver Mire Trailović 1; Tel: 3220-608;
www.bitef.co.yu
Jugoslovensko dramsko pozorište
(drama), Kralja Milana 50;
Tel: 3061-957; www.jdp.co.yu
Madlenianum opera and theatre
(opera, ballet), Glavna 32, Zemun; Tel: 3162-533; www.madlenianum.co.yu
Malo pozorište "Duško Radović"
(children's theatre and evening stage), Aberdareva 1; Tel: 3232-072
Narodno pozorište, Trg Republike 1
(drama, opera, ballet); Tel: 2620-946;
www.narodnopozoriste.co.yu
Pozorište na Terazijama (musical),
Terazije 29; Tel: 3229-943
Pozorište Slavija (comedy), Svetog Save 16; Tel: 2436-995
Zvezdara teatar (drama, comedy),
Milana Rakića 38; Tel: 2419-664;
www.zvezdarateatar.co.yu

Before going to the ticket-office, check the working hours by phone. The ticket-offices of Belgrade theatres usually work in split shifts. Tickets for the majority of theatres can be bought in "Bilet servis" on Republic Square.

Floral Delivery

Teleflora, Svetogorska 11; Tel: 3030-047, 3030-048, www.teleflora.co.yu

Other

www.beograd.org.yu
Interactive map of Belograde:
www.planplus.co.yu
Belgrade Fair - www.sajam.co.yu

Short Dictionary

Serbian language is difficult to learn and has complicated grammar. Words and phrases we listed here will help you manage in different situations. Do not worry much about the pronunciation, no one will laugh at you for being a foreigner. Still, first try to ask in English since the majority of Belgraders understand and speak it sufficiently. Apart from English, you can try asking in Spanish, Russian, German and French, too.

The only Serbian word accepted in most languages in the world is "**vampir**" (Serbia is the native country of vampires). In some far-away parts of the country the "conscientious" citizens still unearth their late neighbours and drive hawthorne stakes through their hearts in order not to disturb their widows any more.

(translation	word in Serbian	pronunciation)
Love	Ljubav	/lyoo-bahv/
Happiness	Sreća	/sre-cha/
Yes	Da	/dah/
No	Ne	/neh/
Thank you	Hvala	/hvah-lah/
Good morning	Dobro jutro	/doh-broh yoo-troh/
Good afternoon	Dobar dan	/doh-bar daan/
Good evening	Dobro veče	/doh-broh ve-che/
Hello	Zdravo	/zdrah-voh/
Goodbye	Doviđenja	/doh-vee-gi-enya/
Good night	Laku noć	/lah-koo noch/
Tomorrow	Sutra	/soo-trah/
Yesterday	Juče	/yoo-cheh/
When?	Kada?	/kah-dah/
Where?	Gde?	/gh-deh/
What time	Koliko je	/koh-lee-koh
is it?	sati?	ye sah-tee/
Let's go!	Idemo!	/ee-deh-moh/
How are you?	Kako si?	/kah-koh see/
Nice to meet you!	Drago mi je!	/drah-goh mee yeh/
See you!	Vidimo se!	/vee-dee-moh se/
May I...?	Da li mogu... ?	/dah lee moh-ghoo/
Please	Molim Vas	/moh-leem vahs/
Excuse me, Pardon	Izvinite	/eez-vee-nee-teh/
I don't understand	Ne razumem	/neh rah-zoo-mehm/
Good	Dobro	/doh-broh/
Bad	Loše	/loh-sheh/
Big	Veliko	/veh-lee-koh/
Small	Malo	/mah-loh/
Full	Puno	/poo-noh/
Empty	Prazno	/prah-znoh/
Hot	Vruće	/vroo-cheh/
Cold	Hladno	/hlah-dnoh/
More	Više	/vee-sheh/
Less	Manje	/mah-nyeh/
A lot	Mnogo	/mnoh-goh/
A little	Malo	/mah-loh/
Open	Otvoreno	/oh-tvoh-reh-noh/
Closed	Zatvoreno	/zah-tvoh-reh-noh/
In front of	Ispred	/ees-prehd/
Behind	Iza	/eez-ah/
Above	Iznad	/eez-nahd/
Below	Ispod	/ees-pohd/
You	Ti	/tee/
I	Ja	/yah/
We	Mi	/mee/
You	Vi	/vee/
He	On	/ohn/
She	Ona	/ohnah/
They	Oni	/ohnee/
Man	Čovek	/choh-vehk/
Woman	Žena	/zheh-nah/
Young man	Momak	/moh-mahk/
Young woman	Devojka	/deh-voy-kah/
Girl	Devojčica	/deh-voy-chee-tzah/

Boy	**Dečak**	/**deh**-chahk/
May I help you?	**Izvolite**	/eez-**voh**-lee-teh/
Here you are	**Izvolite**	/eez-**voh**-lee-teh/
Room	**Soba**	/**soh**-ba/
Food	**Hrana**	/**hrah**-nah/
Drink	**Piće**	/**pee**-che/
Have a nice meal	**Prijatno**	/**pree**-yat-no/
Breakfast	**Doručak**	/**doh**-roo-chahk/
Lunch	**Ručak**	/**roo**-chahk/
Dinner	**Večera**	/**veh**-cheh-rah/
Bread	**Hleb**	/hlehb/
Salt	**So**	/soh/
Pepper	**Biber**	/**bee**-behr/
Vinegar	**Sirće**	/**seer**-cheh/
Water	**Voda**	/**voh**-dah/
Wine	**Vino**	/**vee**-noh/
Beer	**Pivo**	/**pee**-voh/
Brandy	**Rakija**	/**rah**-kee-yah/
Coffee	**Kafa**	/**kah**-fah/
Tea	**Čaj**	/chahy/
Milk	**Mleko**	/**mleh**-koh/
Salad	**Salata**	/**sah-lah-tah**/
Soup	**Supa**	/**soo**-pah/
Meat	**Meso**	/**meh**-soh/
Fish	**Riba**	/**ree**-bah/
Cheese	**Sir**	/seer/
Eggs	**Jaja**	/**yah**-yah/
Fruit	**Voće**	/**voh**-cheh/
Fruit preserves	**Slatko**	/**slaht**-koh/
Bill	**Račun**	/**rah**-choon/
I'm hungry	**Gladan sam**	/**glah**-dahn sahm/
I'm thirsty	**Žedan sam**	/**zheh**-dahn sahm/
How much is it?	**Koliko košta?**	/koh-**lee**-koh **koh**-shtah/
Can I pay by credit card?	**Može kartica?**	/**moh**-zheh **kahr**-tee-tzah/
Where is the toilet?	**Gde je toalet?**	/gdeh yeh toh-ah-**leht**/
Toilet paper	**Toalet papir**	/toh-ah-**leht pah**-peer/
Bank	**Banka**	/**bahn**-kah/
Post office	**Pošta**	/**poh**-shtah/
Exchange office	**Menjačnica**	/**meh**-nyah-chnee-tzah/
Stamp	**Marka za pismo**	/**mahr**-kah zah **pee**-smoh/
Credit	**Dopuna za telefon**	/**doh**-poo-nah zah teh-**leh**-fohn/
PAYG number	**Pripejd broj za telefon**	/**pree**-peid brohy zah teh-**leh**-fohn/
Hospital	**Bolnica**	/**bohl**-nee-tzah/
Pharmacy	**Apoteka**	/ah-poh-**teh**-kah/
I'm not feeling well	**Nije mi dobro**	/**nee**-yeh mee **doh**-broh/
I have a stomachache	**Boli me stomak**	/**boh**-lee meh **stoh**-mahk/
I have a headache	**Boli me glava**	/**boh**-lee meh **ghlah**-vah/
I have a toothache	**Boli me zub**	/**boh**-lee meh zoob/
Call a doctor!	**Zovite doktora!**	/**zoh**-vee-teh **dohk**-toh-ra/
Road	**Put**	/poot/
Street	**Ulica**	/**oo**-lee-tzah/
Sign	**Znak**	/znahk/
Bridge	**Most**	/mohst/
Petrol	**Benzin**	/**behn**-zeen/
Bus	**Autobus**	/ah-oo-**toh**-boos/
Tram	**Tramvaj**	/**trahm**-why/
Trolleybus	**Trolejbus**	/troh-**lehy**-boos/
Plane	**Avion**	/**ah**-vee-on/
Airport	**Aerodrom**	/ah-eh-roh-**drohm**/
Train	**Voz**	/vohz/
Stop	**Stanica**	/**stah**-nee-tzah/
Bus station	**Autobuska stanica**	/ah-oo-**toh**-boos-kah **stah**-nee-tzah/
Railway station	**Železnička stanica**	/**zheh**-leh-znee-chkah **stah**-nee-tzah/
Customs	**Carina**	/**tzah**-ree-nah/
Port	**Luka**	/**loo**-kah/
Ticket	**Karta**	/**cahr**-tah/
Exit	**Izlaz**	/**eez**-lahz/
Entrance	**Ulaz**	/**oo**-lahz/
Right	**Desno**	/**des**-noh/
Left	**Levo**	/**le**-voh/
Straight	**Pravo**	/**prah**-voh/
Petrol station	**Benzinska stanica**	/**behn**-zeen-skah **stah**-nee-tzah/

I've got a flat tire	Pukla mi guma	/**pook**-lah mee **goo**-mah/
Which bus goes to...?	Koji autobus ide do...?	/**koh**-yee ah-oo-**toh**-boos ee-deh doh.../
Could you call me a taxi, please?	Molim Vas, pozovite mi taksi	/**moh**-leem vahs, poh-**zoh**-vee-teh mee **tahk**-see/

Minute	Minut	/**mee**-noot/
Hour	Sat	/saht/
Half an hour	Pola sata	/**poh**-lah **sah**-tah/
Now	Sada	/**sah**-dah/
After	Posle	/**poh**-sleh/
Monday	Ponedeljak	/poh-**neh**-deh-lyahk/
Tuesday	Utorak	/oo-toh-rahk/
Wednesday	Sreda	/**sreh**-dah/
Thursday	Četvrtak	/cheh-**tvr**-tahk/
Friday	Petak	/**peh**-tahk/
Saturday	Subota	/**soo**-boh-tah/
Sunday	Nedelja	/**neh**-deh-lyah/
January	Januar	/**yah**-noo-ahr/
February	Februar	/**feh**-broo-ahr/
March	Mart	/**mahr**-t/
April	April	/**ahp**-reel/
May	Maj	/**mahy**/
June	Jun	/yoon/
July	Jul	/yool/
August	Avgust	/**ahv**-goost/
September	Septembar	/sehp-**tehm**-bahr/
October	Oktobar	/ohk-**toh**-bahr/
November	Novembar	/noh-**vehm**-bahr/
December	Decembar	/deh-**tzehm**-bahr/

first	prvi	/**pr**-vee/
second	drugi	/**droo**-ghee/
third	treći	/**treh**-chee/
fourth	četvrti	/**cheht**-vr-tee/
fifth	peti	/**peh**-tee/
sixth	šesti	/**shehs**-tee/
seventh	sedmi	/**sehd**-mee/
eight	osmi	/**ohs**-mee/
ninth	deveti	/**deh**-veh-tee/
tenth	deseti	/**deh**-seh-tee/

1 - /**yeh**-dahn/
2 - /dvah/
3 - /tree/
4 - /**cheh**-tee-ree/
5 - /peht/
6 - /sheh-st/
7 - /**seh**-dahm/
8 - /**oh**-sahm/
9 - /**deh**-vet/
10 - /**deh**-set/
11 - /yeh-**dah**-nah-est/
12 - /**dvah**-nah-est/
13 - /**tree**-nah-est/
14 - /cheh-**tr**-nah-est/
15 - /**pet**-nah-est/
16 - /**shes**-nah-est/
17 - /seh-**dahm**-nah-est/
18 - /oh-**sahm**-nah-est/
19 - /deh-**veht**-nah-est/
20 - /**dvah**-deh-set/
30 - /**tree**-deh-set/
40 - /cheh-tr-**deh**-set/
50 - /peh-**deh**-set/
60 - /shehz-**deh**-set/
70 - /seh-dahm-**deh**-set/
80 - /oh-sahm-**deh**-set/
90 - /deh-veh-**deh**-set/
100 - /stoh/
500 - /**peht**-stoh/
1000 - /**hee**-lyah-doo/

Two days in Belgrade

How to make the best of two days in Belgrade?

If you are just passing through Belgrade or staying for the weekend and you want to spend the time the best you can, here is our recommendation for a two-day stay. Start with a walk through the centre, to feel the rhythm and the smell of the city and to meet Belgraders. We suggest starting from Terazije, along Knez

Mihailova Street to Kralja Petra Street. There turn left and take a lunch break in "?" Inn (you've probably become hungry coming to Belgrade; you will need strength for the rest of the day). Try veal pottage, meat balls on kajmak and domestic coffee. Since you are already there, visit Princess Ljubica's Residence, where you will see some of Belgrade's interior decorations from the 19th century. Afterwards, take a stroll down Kosančićev venac, to feel the cobblestones underneath your feet and the spirit of old Belgrade. Continue the walk in Kalemegdan Park and visit the Belgrade Fortress. If your

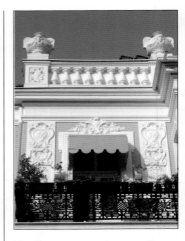

blood pressure gets low, a coffee on "Kalemegdanska terasa" and a view over the Sava-Danube confluence will refresh you. Don't miss the sunset from the plateau around the Belgrade "Pobednik" Monument, especially if you are with your loved one (very romantic).

→ *More information on Belgrade Fortress and the history of Belgrade on page 33.*

From Kalemegdan Park go straight to Strahinjića Bana Street, the place where the fun starts in Belgrade. Take a stroll through it and choose a café that suits you best for a drink or two before dinner. From there the road leads you straight to Skadarlija, an old bohemian quarter.

Have dinner in one of the authentic Belgrade inns (smoked carp or something grilled), with the sounds of old town music. For an aperitif try one of the domestic brandies. Eat well because the night is long.

If you are still able to stand on your own feet, take a taxi to "Crni Panteri", and if you notice that the raft is packed or that it is sinking, drop into another raft nearby, feel free to experiment. With the first rays of the sun, before going back to the hotel, it is necessary to take a hot burek to compensate for the lost energy.

The next day, after stretching in bed and breakfast in the hotel or in a bakery nearby, it is probably better to relax a bit. Gardoš in Zemun is the right place for that. The morning coffee in "Galerija" and a calming view over the Danube, a stroll down the Danube quay and cakes on "Amsterdam". When you get hungry try other Serbian cuisine specialties in "Zlatnik" Restaurant, one of the best in town. After buying souvenirs and a short rest at the hotel, the time has come for the second night in Belgrade. If it's still not after 8pm, buy something in the chocolate sweets store "Adoré" in "Milenijum" Sho-

pping Centre (e.g. chocolate with chilli or with four kinds of spices, to sharpen the spirit). Start warming up in one of the cafés on Obilićev venac, you might meet someone interesting. A place for getting in good mood is definitely the cocktail bar "Ben Akiba" situated in one of the apartments in Nušićeva Street. If you have entered into the rhythm of Belgrade you will finish the night in "Andergraund" club. Every morning demands the compensation for the lost calories and the right place for that is "Loki", on the corner of Kralja Petra and Jovanova Streets.

Sweet dreams.

The aim of this text was to inspire you to make your own itinerary according to your interests, in order to make the best of a short stay in Belgrade. We are certain that you will enjoy the places we recommended in this guide.

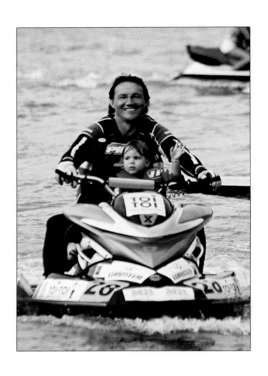

CIP - Katalogizacija u publikaciji
Narodna biblioteka Srbije, Beograd

338.48 (497.11 Beograd) (036)

TASIĆ, Nemanja
How to Conquer Belgrade : complete guide for
getting by in Belgrade / [text Nemanja Tasić ;
photograps Jelena Tasić ; translation into english
Jovana Popović]. - Belgrade : Perollo, 2006
(Belgrade : Portal). - 144 str. : ilustr. ; 21 cm

Kor. nasl. - Tiraž 4.000. - Short Dictionary:
str. 137-139.

ISBN 86-83253-02-3
1. Tasić, Jelena
a) Beograd - Vodiči
COBISS.SR-ID 132550924